Grand Diplôme Cooking Course

Volume 6

Grand Diplôme Cooking Course

A Danbury Press Book

The Danbury Press

a division of Grolier Enterprises, Inc.

Robert B. Clarke   Publisher

This book has been adapted from the Grand Diplôme Cooking Course, originally published by Purnell Cookery, U.S.A.

Purnell Grand Diplôme Editorial Board

Rosemary Hume and Muriel Downes
Principals, London Cordon Bleu Cookery
School, England

Anne Willan	Editor
Eleanor Noderer	Associate Editor
Sheryl Julian	Assistant Editor
John Paton	Managing Editor
José Northey	Co-ordinating Editor
Peter Leather	Art Editor
Charles F. Turgeon	Wine Consultant

Library of Congress Catalog Card Number: 72-13896
© B.P.C. Publishing, 1971, and
© Phoebus Publishing, 1972.
Filmsetting by Petty and Sons Ltd., Leeds, England.
Printed in the United States of America

234567899876543

All recipes have been tested either at the Cordon Bleu Cookery School in London or in our U.S. test kitchens.

Note: all recipe quantities in this book serve 4 people unless otherwise stated.

Contents

From the Editor

From the rich and rustic French countryside, to the sweeping green valleys of our own heartland, whether it be a grand style 'simple' picnic or a hearty winter supper, the many **Menus** for entertaining from the sixth Volume of the Grand Diplôme Cooking Course will hold the stage.

The zesty, robust fragrance of **French Country Cooking**, of garlic, herbs and red wine seasoning a rump or round roast of beef is as bourgeois as the distinctive fisherman's stew from the Mediterranean, bouillabaisse. The colorful **Winter Salads**, composed of escarole and endive or the hearty mixtures of beets and artichokes, will be a favorite accompaniment to one of the delicately light chowders or rich creamy brews suggested by the Cordon Bleu Cookery School of London in the multi-reciped section on **Broth, Cream and Purée Soups**.

For the grand finale, delight your guests while perfecting your skills with assorted sweets of chocolate éclairs and fruit-filled puffs from **Choux Pastry**. Or tempt their palate even further with one of the delicious, feather-light features from the section on **Sponge Cakes**.

To expand your cooking repertoire, you will find invaluable advice on **Choosing and Carving Meat**. This special feature will make you an expert on the basics of beef and veal so you can go on to any dish — from braised brisket to sweetbreads in cream. Then refer to the A to Z of **Freezing** for how to preserve your favorite fruits and vegetables.

Have fun and plan for an encore. Bon Appétit!

Anne Willan

Greek lemon soup is garnished with diamonds of baked egg white, and whipped cream (recipe is on page 10)

AN INTERNATIONAL MENU STARTS WITH GREEK LEMON SOUP

Most of this menu can be prepared well in advance, and the main dish — a sauté of duck served with a rich brown sauce — deserves a high quality, full-flavored red Burgundy. Among the most popular sources of such wines is the little town of Pommard, France, and a good many more bottles labeled Pommard seem to be sold than this place could produce. The wary buyer does well to pay a little extra for those Pommards which specify their origin among the district's top vineyards. Alternatively, you can bypass all these problems and buy a fine Pinot Noir from the San Francisco Bay area.

Greek Lemon Soup (Avgolemono)
or
Sole Orly
with Pimiento Sauce

Sauté of Duck with Burgundy
Sicilian Potatoes
Tomato & Orange Salad

Apple Mousse Gâtinaise
or
Raspberry & Cranberry Compote
with Yogurt Cream

Red wine — Pommard (Côte de Beaune)
or Pinot Noir (California)

TIMETABLE

Day before
Make the chicken stock for the duck and soup.
Make soup but do not add egg yolk liaison; prepare egg white garnish.
Or make fritter batter for sole, cover and refrigerate. Prepare pimiento sauce, cover and refrigerate.

Morning
Prepare the apple mousse and poach apples separately for decoration. Make the caramelized walnuts and store in airtight container.
Or make the raspberry and cranberry compote and chill. Make the yogurt cream and chill.
Brown the duck and let cool. Cut into pieces, complete the cooking and leave to cool. Cover and refrigerate until ready for reheating.
Prepare Sicilian potatoes and leave, covered, on buttered baking sheets ready to be browned.
Put sole fillets on a plate and sprinkle with lemon juice; cover and refrigerate.
If serving soup chilled, reheat, thicken with egg yolk liaison, then cool and chill again in refrigerator.

Assemble equipment for final cooking from 7:15 p.m. for dinner around 8 p.m.

Order of Work

7:15
Set oven at hot (400°F).
Turn out apple mousse and decorate top with walnuts and apples.

7:30
Put Sicilian potatoes in oven to brown, then arrange on a warm platter and keep warm in oven with heat turned off.
Cook green vegetable.
Finish preparing sole fillets.

7:45
Reheat the duck on top of stove over low heat for 10 minutes or until very hot. Arrange on a serving platter and keep warm in the oven.
If the soup is to be served hot, reheat it and thicken with egg yolks. Garnish the soup with the egg white shapes and whipped cream just before serving.
Deep fry the sole fillets and pile on a hot platter.

8:00
Serve appetizer.

You will find that **cooking times** given in the individual recipes for these dishes have sometimes been adapted in the timetable to help you when cooking and serving this menu as a party meal.

Greek Lemon Soup
(Avgolemono)

thinly peeled rind and juice of 1 small lemon
2 tablespoons butter
3 shallots, finely chopped
1½ tablespoons flour
5 cups well-flavored chicken stock
2–3 egg yolks
¼ cup heavy cream, whipped until it holds a soft peak

For garnish
1 egg white
1–2 tablespoons light cream
salt and pepper

Individual soufflé dish or custard cup

This soup may be served hot or chilled.

Method
Melt the butter in a pan, stir in the shallots, cover and cook over a low heat for 2–3 minutes until soft but not browned. Take pan from heat and stir in the flour. Gradually pour in the stock and bring mixture to a boil, stirring constantly. Simmer for 10 minutes and add the lemon rind and strained lemon juice.
Watchpoint: to be sure this soup is not too sharp in flavor, add the lemon juice gradually and taste for sharpness.
Continue to simmer the soup for 7–10 minutes, then strain and rinse pan. Return soup to the pan and set aside.
Set the oven at moderately low (325°F).
To make the garnish: beat the egg white with a fork, enough to break it up, and stir in the light cream with salt

and pepper. Pour mixture into a buttered individual soufflé dish or custard cup and bake in heated oven for 7–10 minutes or until it is firm to the touch. Remove from oven and let stand until cold. Turn out of the dish, slice and cut into tiny rounds or diamonds.
For liaison, mix egg yolks together, stir in a little of the warm soup, then add this mixture to remaining soup. Reheat, stirring constantly, but do not boil or the soup will curdle. Just before serving the hot soup, add the whipped cream and egg white garnish.
If serving the soup chilled, let it cool after heating with the egg yolks, then refrigerate. Add the garnish of egg white and whipped cream just before serving.

Slice the cold, baked egg white and cut into tiny diamonds to garnish the soup

Alternative appetizer

Sole Orly
with Pimiento Sauce

1½ lb sole fillets
squeeze of lemon juice
½ cup seasoned flour (made
    with ½ teaspoon salt and
    ¼ teaspoon pepper)
deep fat (for frying)

For fritter batter
½ cup flour
¼ teaspoon salt
4 egg yolks
2 tablespoons melted butter
    or oil
1 cup milk
2 egg whites

The name Orly usually means fish or meat that is coated with a rich batter, then fried in deep fat until crisp. Any firm white fish fillets such as flounder may be used in this recipe.

Method
Lay the fish on a plate, sprinkle lightly with lemon juice and chill about 1 hour.

To make fritter batter: sift the flour and salt into a bowl, make a well in the center and add the egg yolks and butter or oil. Add the milk gradually, mix to a smooth batter and beat it well. Stand the batter in a cool place (not in refrigerator) for 30 minutes. Just before frying, stiffly whip the egg whites and fold into the batter. Dry the fillets on paper towels and cut in diagonal strips, 1 inch wide.

To fry the fish: first toss in seasoned flour. Heat deep fat to 350°F–365°F on a fat thermometer, or until a 1 inch cube of bread browns in 60 seconds. Drop 6–8 pieces of fish into the batter, turn with a fork to coat all sides and lower carefully into hot fat. Fry until they are golden brown, remove from fat, drain on paper towels and keep warm. Continue with remaining fish and batter. When all the fish is fried, transfer to a serving platter and serve pimiento sauce separately.

Serve sole Orly, crisply fried fillets of sole in batter, with pimiento sauce

Pimiento Sauce

2 slices of canned pimiento,
    drained and finely chopped
    or rubbed through a sieve
1 tablespoon juice from the
    pimientos
2 egg yolks
1 hard-cooked egg yolk,
    worked through a sieve
½ teaspoon paprika
salt and pepper
dash of Tabasco
grated rind of ½ orange
1 cup olive or salad oil
2 teaspoons vinegar (or to taste)
1 tablespoon heavy cream
    (optional)

Method
Combine egg yolks and sieved hard-cooked egg yolk in a bowl. Work in seasonings and orange rind; gradually beat in the oil, drop by drop, as if making mayonnaise. When sauce begins to get very thick, add vinegar, then beat in the remaining oil a teaspoon at a time. Add pimientos after all the oil is mixed in. Thin sauce with a little juice from pimientos and the cream, if needed. Taste and adjust seasoning.

Sauté of duck with Burgundy is garnished with fried croûtes and accompanied by Sicilian potatoes and Brussels sprouts

Entrée

Sauté of Duck with Burgundy

5 lb duck
1 tablespoon oil or butter
2 tablespoons butter (optional)
1 medium onion, thinly sliced
2 cups ($\frac{1}{2}$ lb) small mushrooms
1 cup red Burgundy wine
$\frac{1}{2}$ cup well-flavored chicken
 stock
salt and pepper
kneaded butter (made with
 2 tablespoons butter and
 1 tablespoon flour)
2–3 slices of bread, cut in
 triangles and fried in
 3–4 tablespoons oil and
 butter, mixed, to make
 croûtes (for garnish) –
 optional

This recipe is also good for wild duck.

Method
In a large sauté pan or skillet, brown the duck on all sides in the oil or butter. Be sure to do this slowly for 20–25 minutes over medium heat so that the fat is extracted and the finished dish is not greasy.

Remove the duck from the pan and let cool until it can be handled comfortably. Divide the duck into four, first cutting along the breastbone with a sharp knife. With heavy kitchen shears cut down through breastbone and on either side of the backbone; divide each half in two diagonally between wing and leg. Trim the pieces neatly and set aside (the backbone can be used for stock). Pour the fat from the sauté pan, leaving 2 tablespoons, or if you prefer, use the same amount of butter instead of the fat from the duck. Cook the onion in this until it browns lightly, then add the mushrooms, and sauté briskly for 2–3 minutes until tender.

Heat the wine in a small pan, boil it to reduce by one-third, and add it to the sauté pan with the stock. Cook, stirring constantly, until the mixture boils, season with salt and pepper to taste and put in the pieces of duck. Cover and simmer 15 minutes for slightly pink meat. For an older bird, or if you prefer your duck well done, simmer about 15 minutes longer or until very tender. Trim bones if necessary.

To serve, pile the pieces of duck onto a heated serving platter and keep warm. Whisk small pieces of kneaded butter to thicken it slightly, bring to a boil and simmer 2 minutes. Taste for seasoning and spoon over the duck. As with most sautés, there should be just enough sauce to coat the duck, with about 2 tablespoons extra for each serving.

Garnish the platter with croûtes of fried bread, if you like, and serve with Sicilian potatoes and Brussels sprouts or with tomato and orange salad.

Accompaniments to entrée

Sicilian Potatoes

3–4 medium potatoes
1 small orange
pinch of baking soda
$\frac{1}{2}$ cup butter
2 shallots, finely chopped
salt and pepper
1 egg yolk (optional)

Method
Put the orange in a pan of water with the pinch of baking soda, cover and boil 45–50 minutes. Peel the potatoes, cook in boiling salted water for 15–20 minutes or until tender and drain thoroughly. Mash them with a potato masher or work through a sieve, and transfer to a bowl.

Set the oven at hot (400°F). Drain the orange, cut in quarters and remove all seeds. Chop the quarters, including the rind, very finely. Melt half the butter in a small saucepan, add the shallots and cook until lightly browned. Add the chopped orange and cook, uncovered, for several minutes until fairly dry. Stir the mixture into the potatoes with a fork, season with salt and pepper and beat in 1 tablespoon of the remaining butter and the egg yolk, if used.

Melt remaining butter and brush 2 baking sheets with it. Shape the potato mixture into balls the size of walnuts. Arrange these on the baking sheets, allowing space between each one, and flatten each potato ball with a fork to $\frac{1}{4}$ inch thickness. Bake in heated oven for 10–15 minutes or until well browned Remove baking sheets from the oven and slip a small spatula under each potato cake to loosen it.

Serve Sicilian potatoes, overlapping, on a hot platter with the browned, almost caramelized, underside on top. These crisp potato cakes also make good cocktail hors d'œuvre.

Tomato and Orange Salad

2 tomatoes, peeled and thinly
 sliced
3 oranges
1 teaspoon sugar
$\frac{1}{4}$ cup vinaigrette dressing
 (see page 38)

Method
Sprinkle the sugar over the tomatoes. Thinly peel the rind from 1 orange, cut the strips into needle-like shreds, blanch in boiling water for 1 minute and drain. Cut the remaining rind and pith from the oranges with a serrated-edge knife and section them, discarding the membrane, or slice them.

Arrange the oranges in a serving dish with the tomatoes, spoon over the vinaigrette dressing and scatter the shredded peel on top.

Dessert

Apple Mousse Gâtinaise

8–10 medium tart apples
3 tablespoons butter
grated rind of $\frac{1}{2}$ lemon
2–3 tablespoons honey
1 envelope gelatin
$\frac{1}{4}$ cup cold water
squeeze of lemon juice
1 cup heavy cream, whipped
    until it holds a soft shape
about 12 walnut halves

For syrup
$\frac{1}{2}$ cup sugar
$1\frac{1}{2}$ cups water

8–9 inch moule à manqué pan,
* or deep round mold (1$\frac{1}{2}$ quart*
* capacity)*

This dessert takes its name from the local honey of Gâtinais, near Orleans in France.

Method

Lightly oil the pan or mold. Pare and core 6–7 apples, reserving 2–3, then grate or chop them. Rub 1 tablespoon of the butter around a deep skillet, add apples and cook over a low heat to bring out the juice. Increase heat and cook them, stirring, until pulpy. Add the lemon rind and continue cooking, stirring, until the apples are a thick purée. Remove from heat, add honey to taste and stir until well mixed.

Sprinkle the gelatin over the cold water and lemon juice, stand 5 minutes until spongy, and then dissolve over a pan of hot water. Stir into the apple mixture and set aside to cool. When almost cold, carefully fold the whipped cream into the apple mixture. Spoon into the oiled pan or mold and refrigerate for 2 hours or until the mousse mixture is firm.

To make the syrup: heat sugar and water together in a pan until sugar is dissolved and bring to a boil. Pare the remaining apples, quarter and core them and poach in the sugar syrup for 7–10 minutes or until just tender. Cool in the syrup with the lid on the pan (this helps the apples become translucent in appearance). Drain and set aside, leaving syrup in the pan.

Add the remaining 2 tablespoons butter to the syrup and boil rapidly until the mixture is reduced to a caramel. Dip the bottom of the pan in cold water to stop the mixture cooking and drop in the walnut halves. Turn them around gently so they are coated with caramel on all sides, then lift out with a spoon onto an oiled pan or plate.

To serve: unmold the mousse onto a platter and arrange the apple quarters and caramelized walnuts on top.

Apple mousse gâtinaise is ▶ *decorated with caramelized walnuts and poached apple quarters*

Carefully fold the cream, ▶ *whipped until it holds a soft shape, into the apple and honey mixture*

Coat the walnut halves with ▶ *caramel to make the decoration for apple mousse gâtinaise*

Raspberry and cranberry compote is served with yogurt cream separately

Alternative dessert

Raspberry and Cranberry Compote
with Yogurt Cream

1 package frozen raspberries, thawed
2 cups ($\frac{1}{2}$ lb) cranberries
$\frac{1}{2}$ cup sugar
3 tablespoons port or sweet sherry (optional)

For yogurt cream
1 cup vanilla yogurt
$\frac{1}{2}$ cup heavy cream, whipped until it holds a soft shape

Method
Drain the raspberries; put them and the juice in a pan with the cranberries. Cover and simmer 5 minutes or until the berries are just tender. Add the sugar, stir gently and let cool. Add the port or sherry, if used, and chill.

To make the yogurt cream: stir the yogurt to soften it slightly, then fold in the whipped cream and chill.

Serve yogurt cream separately with the compote.

Rib roast of beef is served with french fries

HOW TO CHOOSE & CARVE MEAT (1) BEEF & VEAL

Meat is the most expensive item on any food budget and everyone wants the best value for the money.

The quality of a carcass is indicated by the U.S. Department of Agriculture (USDA) grades that are stamped on most pieces of meat, although the mark is often cut off during trimming.

The top grades of beef, Prime and Choice, have plenty of fat marbling the lean to give flavor and tenderness. The middle grades, Good and Standard, are reliable for pot roasting and braising. The bottom grades, Commercial and Utility, are rarely sold in retail markets because they lack tenderness. Lamb is divided into five similar grades; veal and pork are not usually graded, though they are inspected.

As well as quality, it is essential to know about the cuts of meat and how each one should be treated. To get an idea of the size and shape of pieces of meat, look at our charts showing how the retailer divides an animal; then go on to read the best way to cook each cut.

This lesson describes how to choose and carve the most familiar cuts of beef and veal; lamb, pork and ham will be discussed in Volume 7. For how to roast meat, see Volume 1.

REGULAR ROASTING TIMES FOR MEAT

TOTAL COOKING TIME (all at 375°F oven temperature)	On meat thermometer
Beef	
Rare: 15 minutes per lb plus 15 minutes more	140°F
Medium: 18 minutes per lb plus 20 minutes more	160°F
Well done: 20 minutes per lb plus 30 minutes more	170°F
Veal	
Well done: 25 minutes per lb plus 25 minutes more	175°F

Points to remember

1 Only the best cuts of the top grades can be cooked quickly with high heat by broiling or roasting. As a general rule, the cheaper the cut, the more slowly it should be cooked, so that the heat and moisture have time to make meat tender. Pot roasting or braising is ideal for less tender meat and flavor can be added with ingredients like stock, wine, tomatoes, peppers or mushrooms.

2 The cheapest cuts often contain a large proportion of bone and make good soup; don't discard any meat on bones — it will be tender and full of flavor after simmering in water with vegetables and seasoning.

3 The price of cuts decreases as the amount of bone included increases, so you will need a proportionately larger piece.
Allow $\frac{1}{4}-\frac{1}{3}$ lb of lean, boneless meat per person for roasts or stew meat. If it contains some fat or if you are catering for large appetites,

you may need $\frac{1}{2}$ lb per person. For meat with some bone, including rib roasts, boneless steaks, chops and ham, allow $\frac{1}{2}-\frac{3}{4}$ lb per person; for cuts like lamb or veal riblets, allow up to 1 lb.

4 When choosing meat, be sure it is thoroughly trimmed of waste and excessive fat — it is worth going to a good meat man, even if his prices are slightly higher, because the meat will be trimmed properly.
Good carving is essential to good cooking, because no matter how carefully you may cook a piece of meat, some will be wasted if it is not skillfully carved. No special knowledge is needed to slice a rolled roast, but many connoisseurs agree that meat cooked on the bone is more juicy and tender. Also, bones help to prevent meat from shrinking during cooking.
The first step to good carving is understanding the structure of the piece of meat, so if faced with an unfamiliar cut, examine it carefully before it is cooked. Try to research the correct way to

carve it and, whenever possible, watch the experts at work in restaurants.
Decide on a plan of action before you make the first cut — there are two general principals when carving: take the knife right down to the bone, cutting away the slices cleanly so no wasted chunks are left, and (with very few exceptions) slice all cuts of meat across the grain.

Carving Tools

Good sharp knives are really essential if you want to carve well; there are several sizes.

1 A long, broad-bladed knife, often slightly curved. This is used for large cuts like rolled ribs of beef or a boneless ham.
2 Knife with a shorter blade for cuts on the bone, including rib of beef and leg or shoulder of lamb.
3 Poultry or game knife with a comparatively short blade.
4 Ham knife, which is long and narrow; only necessary for whole hams.
(The last two knives are helpful, but not essential.)
If you use too large a knife for a small cut, the knife is clumsy and hard to handle. When possible, all these knives should have a carving fork (with a guard to catch the knife if it slips), in the right proportion to the knife.
Knives may be made of good quality **carbon** or **stainless steel**. Stainless steel is practical as it is easy to clean, but it is difficult to keep the blade very sharp at home. Most professional chefs swear by the traditional carbon steel blades because they can

be easily honed to a razor-sharp edge and sharpened at home. To clean them, rub with a raw potato or with a cloth dipped in an abrasive cleaner, or with fine emery paper. Dry quickly and thoroughly or they will rust; if they do, burnish the blade with steel wool.

Special sharpeners are available for stainless steel, and a straight steel is best for carbon steel knives — avoid using a coarse carborundum stone for fine carbon steel blades.

Electric sharpeners can be used for both stainless and carbon steel knives, but they wear the knives down very fast and it is hard to prevent the edge of the knife from developing a curve so it will not chop well on a flat board.

Electric carving knives are becoming more and more popular. They are excellent for boned cuts, because the knife can run straight down through the meat, and good for dishes that fall apart easily like beef Wellington (fillet of beef in pastry). However, considerable skill is needed to use them for a cut with complicated bones like a leg of lamb.

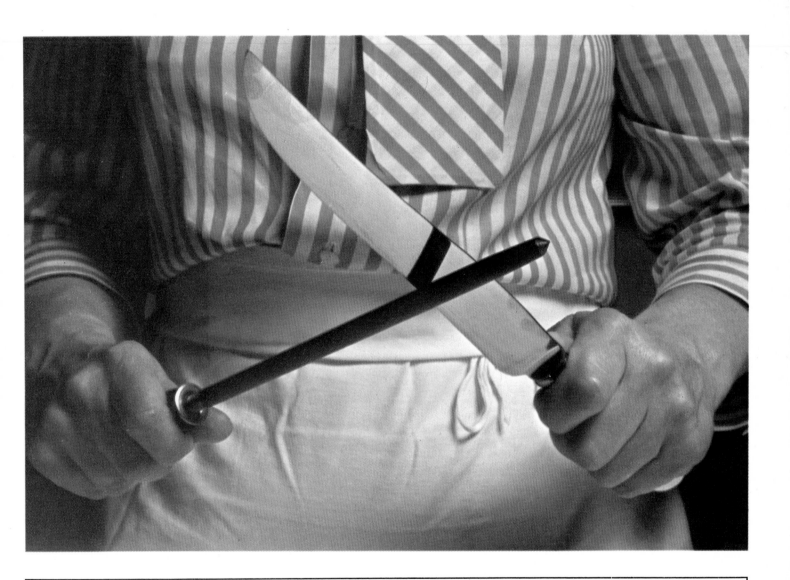

To Sharpen Carbon Steel Carving Knives

If using a steel, hold it in your left hand (if you are right-handed), slanting up, and hold the knife in your right hand. Draw it rapidly up and down the steel on one side, then on the other, with the knife slanting in very slightly and running the steel along the whole length of the blade. Avoid an angle that is too acute or the cutting edge of the knife will be too directly in contact with the steel and the knife will get blunter, not sharper. To get the right idea, watch a butcher sharpen his knives. A carbon steel knife can also be sharpened on a fine carborundum stone: dip stone in water and use exactly the same movement as if you were using a steel.

A simpler way to sharpen a carbon steel knife is to draw the knife away from you 10–12 times up the steel or carborundum stone. Then turn the knife over and draw it towards you in the same way, always keeping the cutting edge away from you and the knife almost flat on the steel or stone.

BEEF

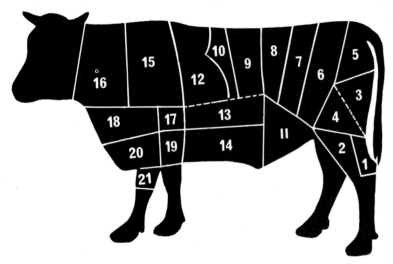

Choice of Cuts

Beef cuts vary slightly in different parts of the country and often the names given to pieces are not the same, but the general method of dividing the carcass is similar throughout the U.S.

Bargains in steaks and roasts are rare — top quality meat is expensive and generally you will get exactly what you pay for. However, many good meals can be made from middle-priced cuts and you will be better off buying cheaper cuts of higher quality graded meat rather than expensive cuts from the poorer grades.

Fresh beef is bright, but not fiery red with plenty of fat marbling the lean in the more expensive cuts. Beef that is suitable for pot roasting will have less marbling, but flavor and tenderness can be added by barding (wrapping meat in a thin sheet of fat) or larding (inserting strips of fat into meat).

Stew beef is also lean but it should have a certain amount of fat — any excess can be easily trimmed.

Carving Beef

Round
Remove the central leg bone and carve the meat in horizontal or diagonal slices.

Sirloin Tip
Slice vertically straight down through the meat — this cut has no bone.

Rump
The standing rump contains several complicated bones and should always be boned and rolled for roasting.

Fillet
Starting at the wide end of the fillet, cut straight down through the meat, making the slices $\frac{1}{2}$–1 inch thick.

Rib Roast
Cut away backbone if not already removed by butcher. Lay the meat on a platter with the bones to one side and the largest end of the meat down. Holding the knife vertically, cut 1–2 rib bones away and carve the meat in horizontal slices $\frac{1}{4}$–$\frac{1}{2}$ inch thick, as you like. Some restaurants cut the meat in one thick slice, serving it like a steak — allow half a rib per serving when doing this.

Arm Roast
Cut away the rib bones and the central leg bone. Carve the meat in horizontal or diagonal slices across the grain.

Brisket
Cut away the ribs and slice vertically down through meat.

Chuck, or Blade, Roast
The bones will vary in shape depending on the end from which the cut was taken. Carve around the bones as much as possible and slice the meat horizontally or diagonally across the grain.

Steaks
Cut around any bone in the steak and remove it. Trim the fat. Carve the meat in diagonal slices about $\frac{3}{4}$ inch thick and give each person a few slices from each section of the steak. If the steak is less than 1 inch thick, cut vertically in portions.

Flank Steak
Flank is an exception to the rule that all meat must be cut across the grain. Starting at the thin end, carve flank in the thinnest possible slices, cutting with the grain of the meat.

1	Heel of round	11	Flank or flank steak
2	Hind shank	12	Rib roast; rib steak
3	Round roast; round steak	13	Short ribs
4	Sirloin tip roast; sirloin tip steak	14	Short plate
5	Rump roast; rump steak	15	Chuck (blade) roast; chuck (blade) steak
6	Sirloin steak	16	Neck
7	Pin bone sirloin steak	17	English cut
8	Porterhouse steak	18	Shoulder roast; arm roast; arm steak
9	T-bone steak	19	Brisket
6, 7, 8 & 9	Fillet (tenderloin) roast; fillet steak	20	Shank
10	Club or Delmonico steak (rib eye)	21	Cross cut foreshank

Serve rib roast of beef with Yorkshire pudding, Brussels sprouts and roast potatoes

CUT OF BEEF	HOW TO COOK	COOKING AND SERVING SUGGESTIONS
1 Heel of round	Braise or stew	Stew with onions, garlic, red wine
2 Hind shank	Simmer	Use for soup, stock, consommé
3 Round roast	Braise	Hot or cold as bœuf à la mode
Round steak	Stew	Swiss steak; carbonnade flamande
4 Sirloin tip roast	Roast top grades, otherwise braise	Braise provençale style
Sirloin tip steak	Broil top grades, otherwise stew	Broil for kebabs; stew as for round steak
5 Rump roast	Roast top grades, otherwise pot roast or braise	Braise as sauerbraten
Rump steak	Stew	Stew or braise chasseur with mushrooms, garlic and white wine
6 Sirloin steak	Broil or pan fry	Serve with garlic or maître d'hôtel butter; stuff with mushrooms
7 Pin bone sirloin steak	Broil or pan fry	As for sirloin steak
8 Porterhouse steak	Broil or pan fry	Serve with sauce bordelaise; steak au poivre or au naturel
9 T-bone steak	Broil or pan fry	Serve with sauce chasseur or bordelaise
6, 7, 8, 9 Fillet (tenderloin)	Roast	Serve hot with sauce madère or bordelaise; wrap in pastry for beef Wellington; cut up for beef Stroganoff; serve cold in aspic, or with green mayonnaise
10 Club or Delmonico steak (rib eye)	Broil or pan fry	Serve with garlic or maître d'hôtel butter; stuff with oysters for carpetbag steak
11 Flank or flank steak	Broil or braise	Broil, slice thinly, serve with mushroom sauce; stuff, braise as roulades
12 Rib roast	Roast	Serve with Yorkshire pudding, roast potatoes, thin gravy
Rib steak	Broil or pan fry	As for T-bone steak

CUT OF BEEF	HOW TO COOK	COOKING AND SERVING SUGGESTIONS
13 Short ribs	Stew or simmer	Stew with carrots, tomatoes, onion; use for soup; simmer as pot-au-feu or boiled beef; braise
14 Short plate	Stew or simmer	Stew with root vegetables; simmer as pot-au-feu
15 Chuck (blade) roast	Pot roast or braise	New Orleans pot roast
Chuck (blade) steak	Braise or stew	Braised with wine for bourguignon or stew with beer for carbonnade
16 Neck	Stew or simmer	Use for beef stock, pot-au-feu, and bean soup
17 English cut	Stew	As for short plate
18 Shoulder roast	Braise or pot roast	Braise as sauerbraten; use for pot roast diabolo
Arm roast	Braise or pot roast	As above
Arm Steak	Stew	As for round steak
19 Brisket	Braise or simmer	Braise with spices; simmer as boiled beef; pickle for corned beef
20 Shank	Stew or simmer	Stew as goulash; use for soup, stock, consommé
21 Cross cut foreshank	Simmer	Use for soup, stock, consommé
Oxtail	Stew or simmer	Stew with onions, tomatoes, garlic; use for soup
Heart	Braise	Stuff with breadcrumbs and herbs
Tongue	Simmer or braise	Braise with root vegetables; serve hot with sherry or Madeira sauce; simmer, press, chill and serve cold with Cumberland sauce
Kidney	Braise	Braise with mushrooms and port; combine with stew beef in a pie
Tripe	Blanch; stew or fry	Stew à la mode de Caen; fry with onions

VEAL

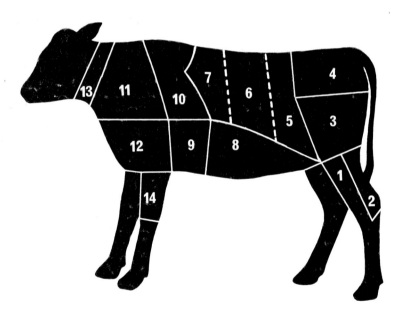

1. Hind shank
2. Heel of round
3. Leg (round) roast, cutlets; escalopes; médaillons; noisettes
4. Rump roast
5. Sirloin roast; sirloin steak
6. Loin chop
7. Kidney chop
8. Flank
9. Breast (riblets)
10. Rib and saddle roast; crown roast; rib chop
11. Shoulder and blade roast; blade steak
12. Arm roast; arm steak
13. Neck
14. Foreshank

Choice of Cuts

Veal is very young beef and the younger the better. Top quality veal is milk-fed and delicate pink in color with a shiny gloss which shows it is freshly cut. It will have little fat.

A calf is smaller than a full-grown beef animal so there are fewer cuts of veal than beef. Many veal cuts can be roasted, but the main problem with veal is lack of flavor, not toughness. The meat dries easily, so roast it French-style with a little stock or wine and cover it with foil or baste it often so that it remains moist. Pan fry rather than broil veal as broiling tends to dry and toughen it.

Veal is usually cooked until it is well done, but some gourmets maintain that roast veal has more flavor it if is a little pink in the center.

Veal roasts are often boned and rolled with or without stuffing as the meat is soft and tends to lose shape unless it is tied. However a few compact cuts are also served on the bone.

For how to roast veal, see Volume 2.

Carving Veal

Rib Roast
Set the roast on a carving board, rib bones pointing up. Cut down between each bone to form chops.

Saddle
This is a double rib roast, joined together by the backbone. Place the saddle on a board, meat side up. Cut along backbone parallel to it and down each side until you reach the ribs. Then carve the meat in $\frac{3}{4}$ inch slices at right angles to the backbone, releasing each slice from the ribs at the bottom before transferring it to a plate.

How to Bone, Stuff and Roll a Breast of Veal Roast

With a short sharp knife, cut out the rib bones from meat

Spread the stuffing evenly on the meat, trim the ends if necessary, then roll up meat to a neat cylinder before tying up with string at intervals

Garnish a rolled stuffed veal roast with cooked red or green bell peppers, if you like

CUT OF VEAL	HOW TO COOK	COOKING AND SERVING SUGGESTIONS
1 Hind shank	Simmer or stew	Use for soup; stew with white wine and tomato for osso buco
2 Heel of round	Pot roast or braise	Pot roast or braise with wine, tomato, herbs, garlic
3 Leg (round) roast	Roast or pot roast	Roast or pot roast with herbs, white wine, lemon
Cutlets	Stew or pan fry	Stew as for sirloin steak; pan fry and serve with mushrooms, artichoke hearts
Escalopes	Pan fry	Serve with lemon, hard-cooked egg, chopped ham, white wine sauce; make into veal birds
Médaillons or noisettes	Braise or pan fry	Serve with sautéed eggplant or tomato; braise with root vegetables, white wine, sherry
4 Rump roast	Roast or pot roast	Sprinkle chopped parsley, grated Parmesan cheese and breadcrumbs on surface 30 minutes before end of cooking
5 Sirloin roast	Roast or pot roast	As for rump roast
Sirloin steak	Stew or pan fry	Serve with mushroom sauce or sauce soubise
6 Loin chop	Stew or pan fry	Stuff chops with duxelles – chopped mushrooms, onions, and shallots; serve with white wine and cream sauce
7 Kidney chop	Pan fry	Serve with maître d'hôtel butter
8 Flank	Braise	Braise with red or white wine, baby onions and carrots
9 Breast	Roast or pot roast	Bone and stuff with lemon, herb, or ham and sausage stuffing and make thin gravy
Riblets	Stew	Stew with baby onions and potatoes and make a sauce with sour cream

CUT OF VEAL	HOW TO COOK	COOKING AND SERVING SUGGESTIONS
10 Rib and saddle roast	Roast	Sprinkle with rosemary, thyme, lemon before cooking
Crown roast	Roast	Fill center with rice and pistachio, or pecan, stuffing
Rib chop	Stew or pan fry	As for sirloin steak
11 Shoulder and blade roast	Pot roast	Pot roast or braise with garlic, herbs, white wine or vermouth and add prunes or olives for garnish
Blade steak	Braise or simmer	Braise as for flank; simmer for blanquette de veau
12 Arm roast	Pot roast or braise	As for blade roast and steak
Arm steak	Braise or simmer	As for blade steak
13 Neck	Simmer	Use for soup
14 Foreshank	Stew or simmer	Use for soup; stew for osso buco
Sweetbreads	Blanch, then braise or pan fry	Pan fry in butter, serve with béarnaise sauce; braise with root vegetables and sherry, or serve in white wine sauce with mushrooms
Kidneys	Broil, pan fry or braise	Broil or pan fry in butter, serve with maître d'hôtel butter; braise with mushrooms and red wine
Brains	Blanch; broil, pan fry or braise	Broil or pan fry and serve with beurre noir; braise with mushrooms and port
Liver	Broil, pan fry or roast	Broil and serve with bacon, mushrooms, etc; braise with mushrooms, onions, red wine
Heart	Braise	Stuff with breadcrumbs and herbs, or rice, or olive and lemon stuffing

Vinaigrette salad is ideal for using up leftovers of cooked meat or fish (recipe is on page 30)

WINTER SALADS

Cold weather shouldn't mean the end of salads, even though summer greens are in short supply. Many winter vegetables like cabbage, escarole, endive and chicory make excellent salads, and hearty mixtures of cooked beets, potatoes, cauliflower, artichokes or apples are particularly welcome in winter.

Some simpler mixtures are best served as side salads with an entrée, but many of the following salads are substantial enough to serve as an appetizer or a light lunch or supper dish.

Vinaigrette Salad

4–5 medium potatoes
2 cups diced cooked beets
3–4 stalks of celery, diced
1 large apple, pared, cored and diced
1 large dill pickle, diced
salt and pepper
1 cup cooked green peas
1½ cups cooked meat, chicken, shellfish or fish, cut in strips or flaked
¾ cup vinaigrette dressing
1–1½ cups mayonnaise
lettuce or chicory leaves

For garnish (optional)
sliced dill pickle
celery curls
cooked, peeled shrimps
sliced salami

This salad is ideal for using up leftovers of cooked meat and fish. Unless seafood is added, this salad is best made a day ahead so the flavors can blend well. It will keep, covered, 2–3 days in the refrigerator. If using shellfish or fish, keep the salad only 1 day.

Method
Cook potatoes in their skins in boiling salted water for 10–15 minutes, drain, peel and dice while still warm. Mix thoroughly with the beets, celery, apple and dill pickle and season well. Stir in peas and meat, chicken, shellfish or fish with a fork. Spoon over the vinaigrette dressing, cover, chill 2–3 hours or overnight.

To serve, arrange a few lettuce or chicory leaves around a salad bowl, toss salad with mayonnaise and spoon into bowl.

If you like, decorate with sliced dill pickle, celery curls, shrimps or sliced salami.

Bean Salad

1 cup (¼ lb) dried red kidney beans, soaked overnight
bouquet garni (made with 1 bay leaf, stalk of celery, 4–5 parsley stalks)
salt
1 medium onion, finely sliced
2 medium tomatoes, peeled, seeded and cut in strips
½ cup (2 oz) hard cheese, preferably Gouda or Edam, cut in strips
2 teaspoons chopped parsley
black pepper, freshly ground
½ cup vinaigrette dressing

Method
Drain the beans, cover with cold water and add bouquet garni and a little salt. Bring to a boil very slowly, cover the pan and simmer 1 hour or until the beans are tender. To test, lift a few out on a spoon; if they burst when you blow on them, they are done. Cool beans slightly in the liquid, then drain.

Cook the onion in boiling salted water for 3–4 minutes until just tender, then drain. Put the beans in a salad bowl with the onion, tomatoes, cheese, parsley and seasoning to taste. Spoon over the vinaigrette dressing, cover and chill at least 2–3 hours so the flavors blend.

To make celery curls: cut thin strips from the sides of celery stalks with a vegetable peeler. Let stand in ice water for 1 hour or until curled.

Leek and Egg Salad

8-10 small leeks
3 hard-cooked eggs, peeled
salt
¼ cup vinaigrette dressing
1–1½ cups mayonnaise
½ teaspoon paprika (optional)

Method
Trim the leeks, split in half lengthwise and wash very thoroughly. Tie them in a bundle and cook in boiling salted water for 10–12 minutes or until just tender. Drain, refresh with cold water and drain again. Untie them, arrange in a serving dish and spoon over the vinaigrette dressing.

Cut the egg whites into strips and sprinkle over the leeks. Work the yolks through a sieve. Thin the mayonnaise, if necessary, with 1–2 tablespoons boiling water and spoon over the salad to coat it. Scatter the sieved yolks on top and sprinkle with paprika, if you like. Cover and chill not more than 1–2 hours before serving.

Quantities in these salad recipes are enough to serve 4 people as a side salad or 2 as an entrée.

Recipes for Salad dressings are given on page 38.

Artichoke and Tomato Salad

1½ lb Jerusalem artichokes
4–5 medium tomatoes, peeled, seeded and cut in strips
salt
squeeze of lemon juice

For yogurt dressing
1 cup plain yogurt
2–3 tablespoons heavy cream
pepper
1 teaspoon sugar
squeeze of lemon juice
2 teaspoons chopped chives or parsley

Jerusalem or root artichokes are no relation to the more familiar spiky globe artichokes, although they have a similar flavor. Root artichokes are available in specialty markets and in some supermarkets.

Method
Peel the artichokes and cut into walnut-size pieces. Cook in boiling salted water to cover, with a squeeze of lemon juice to keep them white, for 10–12 minutes or until just tender. If overcooked, they will become tough again. Drain, refresh and drain again. Put in a bowl with the tomatoes.

To make the yogurt dressing: stir the yogurt into the cream with the seasoning, sugar and lemon juice. Mix gently with the artichokes and tomatoes, reserving a few strips of tomato for garnish.

Arrange the artichoke and tomato salad in a salad bowl or on individual plates, scatter with the reserved strips of tomato and chives or parsley, and serve within 2–3 hours.

Try one of these unusual cooked salads — bean salad; leek and egg (center) or Jerusalem artichoke and tomato salad (far right)

Artichoke and Mushroom Salad

4–6 small fresh artichokes, cooked and halved or 1 can (15 oz) artichoke hearts, drained, or 1 package frozen artichokes, cooked
2 cups ($\frac{1}{2}$ lb) mushrooms, quartered

For dressing
6 tablespoons olive oil
2 tablespoons lemon juice
1 teaspoon tarragon
1 tablespoon chopped parsley
salt
black pepper, freshly ground

Method
To make the dressing: combine all ingredients in a bowl and season to taste. Spoon dressing over the mushrooms, cover and leave 1–2 hours. Add the artichoke hearts, mix well and chill 1–2 hours before serving.

Fresh Artichoke Hearts

Fresh small artichokes are sometimes available in Italian markets. They are completely edible with no hairy choke and have a delicious nutty flavor.

To prepare them, trim the stem, remove any hard outer leaves and trim the tops. Cook in boiling salted water for 15–20 minutes or until tender; drain.

Cauliflower with Mustard Mayonnaise

1 large cauliflower
1 carrot, finely grated
1$\frac{1}{2}$ cups mayonnaise
2 teaspoons Dijon-style mustard
salt and pepper
little milk (optional)
$\frac{1}{2}$ teaspoon paprika

Serve as an appetizer or as a side salad with cold veal or chicken.

Method
Wash the cauliflower, break it into flowerets and cook in boiling salted water for 8–10 minutes or until just tender. Drain, refresh and dry the flowerets thoroughly on paper towels; arrange in a salad bowl.

Fold the grated carrot into the mayonnaise with the seasoning and the mustard and, if necessary, dilute to a coating consistency with a little milk. Spoon the mayonnaise over the cauliflower and sprinkle with paprika. Cover and serve within 1–2 hours.

Quantities in these salad recipes are enough to serve 4 people as a side salad or 2 as an entrée.

Recipes for salad dressings are given on page 38.

Celeriac Rémoulade

1 celeriac (root celery)
salt and pepper

For rémoulade dressing
1 cup mayonnaise
1 teaspoon Dijon-style mustard
$\frac{1}{4}$ teaspoon anchovy paste
2 teaspoons chopped gherkin pickles
1 teaspoon chopped capers
2 teaspoons chopped parsley
1 teaspoon chervil

Serve as an appetizer with sliced salami or as a side salad with cold beef or garlic sausage.

Method
Blanch celeriac in boiling water for 5 minutes to soften the skin, then peel it. Cut into julienne strips, discarding fibrous pieces.
Watchpoint: the celeriac should be firm but not hard when mixed with dressing; if it is very tough it may need blanching again for 1–2 minutes.

Combine all ingredients for rémoulade dressing, mix thoroughly with celeriac and season to taste. Cover and chill at least 3 hours before serving.

Celeriac or root celery is little known here. It is a large nobbly root resembling a rutabaga with a delicious flavor of celery. In France it is often dressed with a tart rémoulade dressing.

Beet, Celeriac and Walnut Salad

Pile celeriac rémoulade in a bowl and arrange slices of cooked beets overlapping around the edge. Sprinkle the center with $\frac{1}{4}$ cup coarsely chopped walnuts and serve.

To Prepare Beets

To boil beets: scrub the beets, taking care not to break the skin. Leave on the roots and about 1 inch of the stems. Cover with cold water and boil 30–60 minutes, depending on age and size of beets. A good test is to remove one of the beets and rub off a small piece of skin. If it comes off easily the beets are cooked. Cool in the cooking liquid, trim off the roots and stems and slip off the skins with your hands.
To bake beets: wash the beets, leave on the roots and 1 inch of stems and wrap in foil. Place in a baking dish and bake in a moderately low oven (325°F) for 30-60 minutes, depending on age and size of beets. Remove roots and stems and, when cool, skin the beets.

Potato salad, on a bed of lettuce, is sprinkled with paprika and garnished with halved ripe olives

Potato Salad

4–5 medium potatoes
¼ cup vinaigrette dressing
salt and pepper
1 cup mayonnaise
1–2 tablespoons light cream
   or milk
½ teaspoon paprika
8–12 ripe olives (for garnish) –
   optional

Method
Cook the potatoes in their
skins in boiling salted water
for 10–15 minutes or until
just tender; do not overcook
or they will break when sliced
and tossed in dressing. While
still hot, peel the potatoes,
cut into slices, add the vinaigrette dressing (potatoes
will absorb it), season, cover
and cool.
   When cold, mix in 2–3
tablespoons mayonnaise and
pile the potatoes in a bowl.
Thin the remaining mayon-
naise with a little cream or
milk and coat the potatoes.
Sprinkle with paprika and
decorate with halved pitted
olives if you like. Cover and
serve within 1–2 hours.

Potato, Celery and Apple Salad

3 medium potatoes
¼ cup vinaigrette dressing
bunch of celery, sliced
1 large tart apple
1 cup lemon cream dressing

Serve with cold cooked meats.

Method
Cook the potatoes in their
skins in boiling salted water
for 10–15 minutes or until
just tender. Drain peel and
slice them while still hot.
Toss the potatoes with vinaigrette dressing and cool.
   Pare, core and slice the
apple and mix with celery
and potatoes and half the
lemon cream dressing. Pile
the salad in a bowl, spoon
the remaining dressing on top
and serve within 1 hour.

Celery, Apple and Walnut Salad

bunch of celery
2 Golden Delicious apples
½ cup walnut halves
½ cup vinaigrette dressing
1 tablespoon chopped parsley

Serve with roast chicken and
pork dishes.

Method
Trim and wash the celery.
Cut into 2 inch sticks, soak in
ice water for 30 minutes
until crisp, then drain and
dry thoroughly. Wipe the
apples, but do not pare. Core
and slice them and mix with
the celery and walnut halves.
   Toss the apple mixture
with vinaigrette dressing and
leave, covered, for 30–60
minutes. Sprinkle the salad
with chopped parsley just
before serving.

Chicory or Escarole Salad

1 head of chicory, or escarole

For dressing
6 tablespoons oil
6 tablespoons white wine
   vinegar or cider vinegar
1 teaspoon Dijon-style mustard
salt and pepper
¼ cup heavy cream

Serve with steak, roast meat
or chicken.

Method
Divide the chicory or escarole
into leaves, wash, drain thoroughly and tear into 2–3
inch pieces. Whisk the ingredients for the dressing until
slightly thickened and toss
with the greens. Serve as
soon as possible.

Carrots in Salad
When cutting julienne
strips or grating raw carrots, use only the outside
orange part unless the
carrot is very young. The
inner yellow core has less
flavor and is often tough.

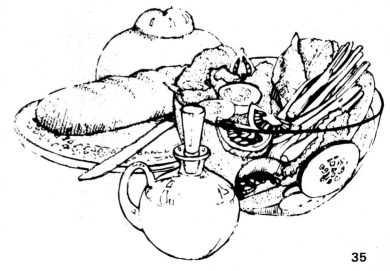

Add a squeeze of lemon juice to vinaigrette dressing for bean, tomato and cucumber salad

Bean, Tomato and Cucumber Salad

¾ lb green beans
4 medium tomatoes, peeled, quartered and seeded
2 cucumbers
squeeze of lemon juice (optional)
¼ cup vinaigrette dressing

Method
Trim the beans, wash them, tie in bundles and cook in plenty of boiling salted water for 15 minutes or until just tender. Drain, refresh and drain again. Peel the cucumbers, cut in quarters lengthwise and cut into small chunks.

Add a squeeze of lemon juice to the vinaigrette dressing, toss a little with the cucumbers and with the tomatoes and spoon some over the beans. Arrange the vegetables on a platter with the beans (strings discarded) in the center, and spoon over any remaining dressing. Chill.

Orange and Pineapple Salad

3 navel oranges
1 medium ripe pineapple
6 tablespoons vinaigrette dressing, preferably made with white wine vinegar
1–2 teaspoons sugar
1 head escarole or Boston lettuce

Method
Cut the rind and pith from the oranges and remove the sections. Cut the skin from the pineapple, remove the core and cut the flesh into chunks the size of the orange sections. Mix the orange and pineapple with the vinaigrette dressing and sugar to taste.

Wash the escarole or Boston lettuce, dry it and arrange it around a salad bowl. Pile the fruit in the center and chill.

Avocado, Orange and Grapefruit Salad

2 ripe avocados
2 navel oranges, peeled
1 grapefruit, peeled
few leaves of chicory or
    escarole

For dressing
6 tablespoons oil
1½ tablespoons lemon juice
1 tablespoon chopped mint
    (optional)
salt and pepper
1–2 teaspoons sugar

Serve with hot or cold roast chicken or duck.

Method
To make the dressing: combine the oil, lemon juice, mint, if using, with the salt, pepper and sugar to taste.

Halve the ripe avocados, remove the seeds and slice. Arrange the chicory or escarole leaves around a large platter, place the avocado slices overlapping just inside the leaves and spoon over a little dressing to prevent the avocado from turning brown.

Section the oranges and arrange them inside the avocado ring. Remove the grapefruit sections and arrange in the center of the platter. Spoon over the remaining dressing and serve as soon as possible.

Quantities in these salad recipes are enough to serve 4 people as a side salad or 2 as an entrée.
Recipes for salad dressings are given on page 38.

COLE SLAW

Cole slaw is generally considered an American recipe but takes its name from the first Dutch settlers who took over Manhattan Island. In Dutch, *kool* means cabbage and *sla* salad.

Cole slaw is not limited to the familiar shredded green cabbage mixed with mayonnaise or vinaigrette dressing. For a change, try one of the following variations. A recipe for regular cole slaw is given on page 98.

Shrimp Cole Slaw

1 small firm head of green
    cabbage, finely shredded
¾ lb peeled, cooked baby
    shrimps
2 hard-cooked eggs, peeled
few leaves of Boston or
    romaine lettuce (to serve)

For dressing
½ cup heavy cream, whipped
    until it holds a soft shape
1 cup mayonnaise
1 teaspoon anchovy paste
salt and pepper

Method
Separate 1 hard-cooked egg and work the yolk through a sieve. Coarsely chop the egg white with the other hard-cooked egg and mix it with the finely shredded cabbage and shrimps.

To make the dressing: fold the cream into the mayonnaise with anchovy paste and season to taste. Toss the dressing with the shrimp and cabbage mixture.

Arrange the lettuce leaves on individual salad plates, pile the cole slaw on top and sprinkle with sieved egg yolk. Serve as soon as possible.

Cheese Cole Slaw

1 firm head of green cabbage,
    finely shredded
¾ cup diced sharp Cheddar
    cheese
4 red apples, wiped, cored and
    diced (unpared)
¼ cup raisins
salt
black pepper, freshly ground
1½ cups mayonnaise
¼ cup coarsely chopped
    walnuts

Method
Toss the cabbage, apples, cheese, raisins and salt and pepper to taste with 1 cup of the mayonnaise. Pile in a bowl, cover and chill 1–2 hours.

Just before serving, coat with the remaining mayonnaise and sprinkle with chopped walnuts.

Cole Slaw with Cream

1 firm head of green cabbage,
    finely shredded
1 tablespoon chopped parsley

For dressing
¾ cup heavy cream, stiffly
    whipped
½ teaspoon celery seed
¾ teaspoon salt
½ teaspoon sugar
¼ teaspoon pepper
1 tablespoon cider vinegar

Method
Toss the shredded cabbage with the chopped parsley.

To make the dressing: add the celery seed, salt, sugar, pepper and vinegar to the whipped cream and pour over the cabbage. Toss until the cabbage is coated and serve as soon as possible.

Savoy Cole Slaw

1 firm head of Savoy cabbage,
    finely shredded
1 teaspoon salt
1 tart apple, pared, cored and
    chopped

For dressing
1 cup sour cream
½ cup tomato juice
1 medium dill pickle, finely
    chopped
2 tablespoons chopped fresh
    dill
½ teaspoon sugar

Method
Sprinkle the shredded cabbage with salt and let stand 30 minutes. Mix the apple with the cabbage.

Combine all the ingredients for the dressing, toss thoroughly with the cabbage mixture and pile into a bowl. Chill 1–2 hours before serving.

Pineapple Cole Slaw

4 slices of pineapple, diced
½ head of green cabbage,
    shredded
2 carrots, grated
½ cup coarsely chopped pecans
    (optional)

For dressing
¾ cup mayonnaise
¾ cup sour cream
2 tablespoons sugar
juice of ½ lemon

Method
Combine the ingredients for the dressing.

Combine the pineapple, cabbage and carrots in a bowl, toss thoroughly with the dressing, cover and chill 1–2 hours before serving.

To serve, pile the pineapple cole slaw in a bowl and sprinkle with chopped pecans.

SALAD DRESSINGS

Vinaigrette Dressing

2 tablespoons vinegar (any of
    the following types: red or
    white wine, cider or tarragon)
½ teaspoon salt
½ teaspoon freshly ground
    black pepper
6 tablespoons oil, preferably
    olive or peanut
1 tablespoon chopped fresh
    herbs (thyme, marjoram,
    basil, or parsley) – optional
pinch of sugar (optional)

Makes ½ cup.

Method
Mix vinegar, salt and pepper
together and gradually add
the oil, whisking until the
mixture thickens. Add the
fresh herbs and sugar, if
you like, and taste for seasoning.

Lemon Cream Dressing

grated rind and juice of 1 lemon
½ cup heavy cream, whipped
    until it holds a soft shape
½ cup mayonnaise
salt and pepper
½ teaspoon prepared mustard

Makes about 1 cup.

Method
Fold the whipped cream
into the mayonnaise. Gradually stir in lemon rind and
juice, season well and add
mustard to taste. Add 1 tablespoon water to thin the dressing, if necessary.

Mayonnaise

2 egg yolks
salt and pepper
pinch of dry mustard
¾ cup oil
2 tablespoons wine vinegar

Makes about 1 cup.

Method
In a bowl beat the egg yolks
and seasonings until thick
with a small whisk or wooden
spoon or use an electric
beater. Add the oil drop by
drop, beating constantly.
When 2 tablespoons of oil
have been added, the mix-
ture should be very thick.
Stir in 1 teaspoon of vinegar.
    The remaining oil can be
added a little more quickly,
either 1 tablespoon at a time
and beaten thoroughly be-
tween each addition until it
is absorbed, or in a thin steady
stream if using an electric
beater. When all the oil has
been incorporated, add remaining vinegar to taste,
with extra salt and pepper if
necessary.
    To thin and lighten mayon-
naise, add a little hot water.
For a coating consistency,
thin with cream or milk.
    If mayonnaise curdles,
start with a fresh yolk in
another bowl. Beat well with
seasoning, then add the curdled mixture to it very slowly
and carefully, as for the oil.
When the curdled mixture is
completely added, more oil
can be beaten in if the mixture is too thin.

Green Mayonnaise

2 tablespoons finely chopped
    parsley
1 tablespoon finely chopped
    chives
1 tablespoon finely chopped
    tarragon
1 teaspoon finely chopped dill
1½ cups mayonnaise

Method
Stir the chopped herbs into
the mayonnaise or purée the
herbs with the mayonnaise
in a blender.
    Cover the mayonnaise and
let stand in a cool place at
least 2 hours for the flavor to
mellow before serving.

Tomato Mayonnaise

To 1½ cups mayonnaise add
1 tablespoon tomato paste or
to taste so the mayonnaise is
well colored and flavored.

Boiled Dressing

1 tablespoon sugar
2 teaspoons flour
1 teaspoon salt
2 teaspoons prepared mustard
1 tablespoon water
½ cup each vinegar and water,
    mixed
1 egg
1 tablespoon butter, softened
2–3 tablespoons light cream
    or milk

This dressing can be kept
covered in the refrigerator
for a few days. Makes about
1½ cups.

Method
Mix dry ingredients, add
mustard and 1 tablespoon
water. Stir into vinegar and
water, bring to a boil, stirring,
and simmer 5 minutes. Beat
egg with butter, pour on hot
vinegar mixture and beat
thoroughly. Cook over very
low heat, stirring constantly,
until the dressing thickens
slightly. Cool. Thin with cream
or milk and mix well.

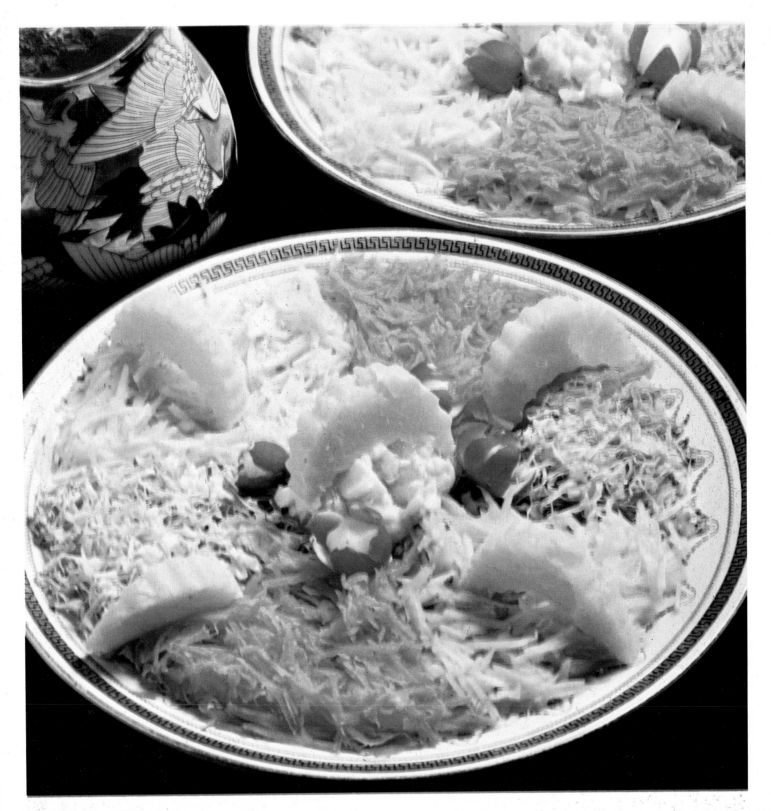

APPLES ARE AN APPETIZER

Stuff apples with celery and serve them with rich cheese pastries for an unusual appetizer. Follow with chicken, cooked with garlic and tomatoes in the style of French Provence. Dessert is a rich cold chocolate soufflé 'raised' in the traditional style by tying a paper collar around the dish.

If your wine merchant can come up with a white or red wine from the Côtes de Provence, by all means try it with this classic Provençal recipe. If not, a rich red Côtes du Rhône or a white Hermitage Blanc from the area just to the north will have the requisite fullness of flavor to match this dish. For an American alternative, pick a Zinfandel from one of the fine California vineyards in the San Francisco Bay area.

Stuffed Apple Salad
with Cheese Sablés

Chicken Provençale
Saffron Rice   *Green Salad*

Cold Chocolate Soufflé

Red wine – Côtes du Rhone (France)
or Zinfandel (California)
White wine – Hermitage Blanc (France)

TIMETABLE

Day before
Prepare and bake the cheese sablés. When cold, store in airtight container.

Morning
Cut the chicken into serving pieces (if whole chicken is used). Prepare the tomatoes for the chicken. Make the soufflé and refrigerate. Do not decorate. Wash the salad greens and store in a plastic bag in the refrigerator. Prepare vinaigrette dressing and store in a jar.
Wash and finely slice the celery and let stand in a bowl of ice water.
Soak the saffron. Cook rice and when drained, store in covered container.
Fry the bacon and crumble. Cook onion for saffron rice and let stand in the pan.

Assemble ingredients for final cooking from 7:00 for dinner around 8 p.m.

You will find that **cooking times** given in the individual recipes for these dishes have sometimes been adapted in the timetable to help you when cooking and serving this menu as a party meal.

Order of Work

7:00
Start to brown chicken. Put plates and serving dishes to warm. Transfer salad greens to a salad bowl ready to add vinaigrette dressing.

7:15
Turn chicken, add remaining ingredients and cook until tender.

7:30
Whip cream, grate chocolate, decorate soufflé and keep in refrigerator.
Prepare the apple salad, arrange it on a serving dish and refrigerate.

7:45
Heat the rice with saffron in pan with onion and butter.
Remove the chicken pieces to warm serving dish and cover with foil. Boil tomato mixture in pan until reduced but do not pour over chicken or sprinkle with chopped herbs until just before serving. Season the rice, add the bacon and spoon into serving dish. Keep warm.
Toss the salad.

8:00
Arrange the cheese sablés around the stuffed apple salad and serve.

Stuffed Apple Salad

4 dessert apples of uniform size
2 stalks of celery, finely sliced
4 walnut halves (for garnish)

For dressing
2 tablespoons heavy cream
2 teaspoons lemon juice or wine vinegar
1 teaspoon sugar (or to taste)
$\frac{1}{2}$ clove of garlic, crushed (optional)
salt
black pepper, freshly ground

Method
Soak the celery in a bowl of ice water so it becomes crisp.

Wipe the apples with a damp cloth and polish them. Slice off the tops and cut out as much of the flesh as possible without breaking the skin. Discard the seeds and cores, chop the flesh and put it in a bowl.

Drain and dry the celery on paper towels, add to the chopped apples and mix well. Stir the cream, lemon juice or wine vinegar, sugar, garlic, if used, and the seasonings together. Pour over the apple and celery mixture and toss carefully until the salad is well coated with dressing. Taste for seasoning.

Watchpoint: if the dressing is stirred too vigorously, it may become too thick and curdle.

Spoon the salad into the apple cases and place a walnut half on the top of each one. Serve with cheese sablés.

Cheese Sablés

$\frac{3}{4}$ cup grated Parmesan or dry Cheddar cheese
$\frac{3}{4}$ cup flour
6 tablespoons butter
salt and pepper
1 egg, lightly beaten

Method
Sift the flour into a bowl. Add the butter, cutting it in with a small spatula, and as soon as the pieces are well coated with flour rub the mixture with your fingertips until it resembles fine breadcrumbs.

Add the cheese and season to taste. Press the mixture together to make a dough. Sprinkle the surface lightly with flour and wrap it in wax paper. Chill at least 30 minutes. Set oven at moderately hot (375°F).

Roll out the dough into a fairly thin oblong with a floured rolling pin. The dough tends to stick, so ease it free from the board with a spatula, if necessary. Cut into strips about 2 inches wide, brush with beaten egg and cut the strips into triangles.

Place these sablés on a baking sheet lined with silicone paper or foil and bake them in heated oven for 12–15 minutes or until golden brown.

Watchpoint: remove baking sheet from oven immediately and lift off the paper with all the sablés on it. Cheese scorches easily and if you remove the sablés one by one, the last ones could become scorched from over-baking.

Serve the sablés cold.

For this menu's appetizer, place cheese sablés on a platter around the stuffed apple salad

Entrée

Chicken Provençale

3½–4 lb roasting chicken, or
    5 chicken pieces (legs,
    thighs, breasts)
¼ cup butter
2 cloves of garlic, peeled
¼ cup sherry or brandy
4–5 ripe tomatoes, peeled,
    seeded and coarsely chopped
1 teaspoon tomato paste
salt and pepper
2 teaspoons chopped parsley
1 teaspoon mixed aromatic
    herbs (marjoram, oregano,
    thyme, basil)

Method
If the chicken is whole, cut it into 5 pieces.

Melt the butter in a skillet or frying pan, add chicken pieces, skin side down, and garlic and cook slowly for about 15 minutes or until the chicken is half cooked.

Turn the chicken pieces over, discard the garlic and add the sherry or brandy. Flame it and when the flame has burned out, simmer until almost all the liquid has evaporated. The chicken should be rich brown.

Add the chopped tomatoes, tomato paste and seasonings to the pan and cook for about 15 minutes longer or until the chicken is tender and the tomatoes are well reduced.

Remove the chicken pieces from the pan, trim them and arrange on a warm platter.

Cook the tomato mixture until it boils and continue boiling until thick. Taste for seasoning. Pour the sauce over the chicken and sprinkle with the chopped parsley and herbs. Serve with saffron rice and a green salad.

Accompaniment to entrée

Saffron Rice

1 cup rice
pinch of saffron, soaked for
    30 minutes in 2 tablespoons
    boiling water
1–2 tablespoons butter
    (optional)
4 slices of bacon
1 small onion, thinly sliced
salt and pepper

Method
Cook the rice in plenty of boiling salted water for about 12 minutes or until tender. Drain in a colander, rinse with hot water and let rice stand until thoroughly drained.

In a frying pan, heat the butter and fry the bacon slices until brown and crisp. Remove them from the pan and drain on paper towels. When cold, crumble the slices into small pieces.

Add the onion to the pan and cook slowly until golden brown. Stir in the rice and add the saffron liquid. With a fork, toss over heat, adding a little butter if necessary to make a rich but fluffy mixture. Season with salt and pepper and stir in the bacon.

Dessert

Cold Chocolate Soufflé

4 squares (4 oz) semisweet
    chocolate, chopped
1½ cups milk
3 eggs
¼ cup sugar
5 tablespoons water or black
    coffee
1 envelope gelatin
¾ cup heavy cream, whipped
    until it holds a soft shape

To decorate
¾ cup heavy cream, stiffly
    whipped
1 square (1 oz) semisweet
    chocolate, grated

Soufflé dish (3 cup capacity);
pastry bag and star tube

Method
To prepare the soufflé dish: make a collar of a double layer of foil or wax or silicone paper and wrap it around the dish, extending it at least 1½ inches above the top of the dish. Attach the paper with string. The soufflé mixture will come above the actual level of the dish, inside the collar, so that when the mixture is set and the paper is removed, the dessert has the traditional 'raised' appearance of a hot soufflé.

Put ½ cup milk into a saucepan with the chocolate. Heat slowly until the chocolate is melted, stirring frequently.
Watchpoint: do not let the milk become more than just warm until the chocolate has melted or the chocolate will be grainy.

Stir the remaining 1 cup milk into the mixture and heat to scalding point. Do not let the mixture boil.

Separate the eggs and beat the yolks with the sugar until thick and light. Gradually stir chocolate-milk mixture into the egg yolks. Return the mixture to the saucepan and cook over low heat, stirring constantly, until the mixture thickens enough to coat the back of a spoon. Do not let the custard boil or it will curdle. Strain it into a large bowl or metal pan and cool, stirring occasionally.

Put the water or coffee in a small pan, sprinkle the gelatin over the top and let stand 5 minutes or until spongy. Stand the pan in a pan of hot water and heat until gelatin is dissolved. Stir quickly into the cold custard.

Beat the egg whites until they hold a stiff peak. Stand the chocolate custard in a pan of ice water and stir frequently until the mixture begins to set. Quickly fold in the lightly whipped cream and egg whites.
Watchpoint: fold in the cream and egg whites as soon as the mixture begins to set or they will not blend completely.

Immediately pour mixture into prepared dish and chill at least 2 hours or until firm.

To decorate: trim the paper collar level with the soufflé mixture. Spread a thin layer of stiffly whipped cream on top of the soufflé and mark it with the point of a knife in a diamond pattern. Put the remaining cream into a pastry bag fitted with a star tube and pipe rosettes around the soufflé. Sprinkle the rosettes with grated chocolate.

Just before serving, remove the paper collar gently from the soufflé by holding the blade of a small spatula in boiling water for a few seconds and then running the blade between the double thickness of paper; the heat loosens it so it peels off easily.

A finished cold chocolate soufflé has the traditional 'raised' appearance of a hot soufflé

Minestrone, a typical Italian soup, is made from a selection of vegetables (recipe is on page 53)

BROTH, CREAM AND PUREE SOUPS

Don't let the convenience of ready-prepared soups deter you from making your own. Soups are one of the simplest and most creative branches of cooking because recipes can be adapted to use almost any available ingredients. Soups are also an excellent way to use up leftovers — even small amounts of cooked or fresh vegetables, poultry and meat will add character to a simple mixture.

Purée and cream soups are cooked quite quickly so they retain their flavor; broths take longer to cook, but are no more trouble as the soup can be left to simmer without harm.

A hearty broth of vegetables, with or without meat, makes a meal in itself if you serve it with a loaf of crusty bread and a wedge of cheese. Purée and cream soups are lighter and more delicate, so they are usually served as an appetizer.

Make soup in large quantities as it can be kept for 3–4 days in the refrigerator and reheats well. If you make soup in advance, do not add cream or a cream and egg yolk liaison until the soup is reheated just before serving. Most soups freeze well, but mixtures containing milk or cream tend to separate when thawed. Bisques, velouté and iced soups were discussed in Volume 3.

Broths

These are thick, hearty soups made from meat or vegetables; they need long simmering over gentle heat to extract the maximum flavor from the ingredients.

Cream Soups

Cream soups are usually made from green vegetables cooked in milk; they are sieved or blended until smooth and thickened with egg yolk and cream. Chicken or veal stock can also be used and this, combined with an egg yolk and cream liaison, gives a velvety consistency, making the classic velouté soups discussed in Volume 3.

Purée Soups

These have a flour, root vegetable or meat base and after cooking they, too, are sieved or puréed in a blender.

Both purée and cream soups are cooked for a relatively short time – 20–40 minutes. They should be sieved or puréed as soon as cooked because standing or prolonged cooking ruins their flavor. It can also spoil their consistency.

However, purée soups based on dried vegetables need long, slow cooking so the vegetables are really soft and almost falling apart before they are sieved or blended.

Note: accompaniments for soups are given on pages 56–57.

Blenders and Sieves

A blender is invaluable for making the smoothest cream and purée soups with a velvety consistency that is almost impossible to achieve by any other method. For best results the mixture should be puréed a little at a time, so that the blender can be turned to high speed.

A food mill is convenient for puréeing soups by hand and is much quicker than using the traditional sieve.

Soups can also be worked through a wire or nylon sieve – this is slow and laborious but results are excellent. Use the rounded side of a wooden spoon when sieving so the maximum surface is in contact with the sieve.

To sieve soup: set food mill or sieve over a bowl and pour the liquid through. Then tip in the food to be sieved a little at a time and work until it is all puréed before adding more. It is important that food is sieved completely, otherwise the soup will lack body and flavor.

To avoid lumps, when sieving a thick soup like potato or bean, strain off the liquid and sieve the solid food into a separate bowl; then dilute the purée gradually with the liquid.

Stocks

The flavor of soup is greatly improved by good stock. For dark vegetable and meat soups you can use either mixed, brown or vegetable stocks; for chicken or light cream soups, use chicken or white stock; and for fish soups, use fish stock.

The basis of an all-purpose mixed stock consists of meat bones or poultry carcasses, or a ham bone, several sliced onions and carrots, a stalk of celery, 6 peppercorns, and a bouquet garni. Put these ingredients in a large kettle, add enough cold water to come about two-thirds above level of ingredients, bring slowly to a boil and skim. Then half cover the pan and simmer $1\frac{1}{2}$–2 hours or longer, depending on quantity of stock being made. The liquid should be reduced by about one-third. Strain off and skim when cold.

Fish stock is made from about 1 lb fish bones, a sliced onion, 6 white peppercorns, a small bouquet garni, juice of $\frac{1}{2}$ lemon, salt and about 5 cups water. Melt about 1 tablespoon butter in a large kettle; add all ingredients except for the water. Place pan, covered, on low heat for 10 minutes. Add water, bring to a boil and skim well. Simmer gently 20 minutes, then strain through a fine nylon sieve before use.

The lesson on making stocks in Volume 2 gave recipes for brown, white, vegetable and mixed stocks.

BROTHS

Simple French Onion Soup

4 medium yellow onions, chopped
3 tablespoons butter
1 tablespoon flour
5 cups stock or water
salt and pepper
1 bay leaf
1–2 dinner rolls, sliced, or 2 slices dry white bread, cut into 4 pieces
$\frac{1}{2}$ cup grated Gruyère or sharp Cheddar cheese

Ovenproof casserole (2 quart capacity), or 4 individual heatproof bowls

Method

In a kettle, heat the butter and, when foaming, add the onions. Lower the heat and cook onions slowly for 15–20 minutes or until golden brown, stirring occasionally with a metal spoon. Stir in the flour, cook 2–3 minutes more until brown and take from heat. Bring the stock or water to a boil, stir into the onion mixture, add seasoning and bay leaf and simmer, uncovered, for 30 minutes. Remove bay leaf.

Lay the sliced rolls or bread in the casserole or bowls and pour in the soup. Sprinkle the top generously with grated cheese and bake in a hot oven (400°F) for 10 minutes or until the cheese is brown. Serve in the casserole or individual bowls.

Watchpoint: the color and flavor of this soup depend on how well the onions are browned – they should be a deep golden but must not be burned. The flavor of the soup is improved by using homemade stock.

Broth, cream and purée soups

Simple French onion soup is topped with grated cheese and browned before serving

Corn chowder is flavored with bacon and onion, and garnished with parsley

Cockie-leekie

5–6 lb fowl
8–12 medium leeks
3–4 quarts cold water
salt and pepper
2 tablespoons rice
1 tablespoon chopped parsley

This Scottish soup is flavored with leeks and traditionally was made with an old cock chicken which gave the soup its name. Cooking times have been adjusted to suit today's relatively tender fowls, so if you use a really tough old bird, simmer it for 1–1½ hours longer.

Method
Place the fowl in a large kettle, add cold water to cover and a large pinch of salt, cover pan and simmer 1 hour.

Trim the leeks, make a deep slit in them lengthwise, wash them thoroughly and slice.

Skim the fat from the pan, add the leeks and rice, cover and continue cooking 1 hour or until the fowl is very tender. Remove it and reserve.

Skim the liquid again; it should be reduced to 8–10 cups. Taste for seasoning and add the parsley. If you like, cut a few slices from the leg of the fowl into julienne strips and add to the soup as garnish.

The fowl can be reheated for another meal and served with a mushroom or curry sauce or with a velouté sauce made with some cooking broth. Or it may be cut up and used for salad, in a mousse or for sandwiches.

Note: accompaniments for soups are given on pages 56–57.

Duck Soup

raw or cooked carcass bones
   and giblets (not liver) of
   1 duck
3½ tablespoons butter
1 onion, sliced
1 carrot, sliced
2 stalks of celery, sliced
bouquet garni
6 cups brown stock or water
salt and pepper
3–4 large mushrooms, sliced
½ cup red wine or ¼ cup sherry
croûtons (for garnish) – optional

For liaison
1½ tablespoons butter
3 tablespoons flour

Carcass bones make excellent soup, particularly if some meat is left on them. If brown stock is not available, add about ½ lb beef shank or a beef bone to the water to strengthen the flavor of the soup.

Method
Cut the duck carcass and neck into medium-sized pieces and, if raw, brown the bones and giblets in 2 tablespoons of the butter in a large kettle. If using beef or beef bones with water as a substitute for brown stock, brown them also. Take the bones and meat from the pan.

Brown the onion, carrot and celery in the butter, add the duck bones, giblets and beef or beef bones (if used), bouquet garni, stock or water, and seasoning. Cover pan and simmer 1–1½ hours.

Strain the soup, cut any duck meat remaining on the bones into shreds and reserve for garnish. Measure the liquid – there should be about 5 cups.

Melt remaining 1½ tablespoons of butter in the pan and sauté the mushrooms until tender. Add the 1½ table-spoons butter for liaison, stir in the flour and add the soup and wine or sherry. Bring to a boil, stirring, and taste for seasoning. Simmer 5 minutes, add the shredded duck and garnish with croûtons before serving.

Corn Chowder

1 cup corn kernels, fresh,
   canned or frozen
¼ lb salt pork, diced
2 tablespoons butter
2 stalks of celery, finely
   sliced
1 onion, finely sliced
2 medium potatoes, diced
2½ cups water
1 bay leaf
salt and pepper
2½ cups milk
1½ tablespoons flour
1 tablespoon chopped parsley
sippets or cheese croûtes
   (for garnish) – optional

Method
Blanch the salt pork; put in cold water, bring to a boil and drain.

In a kettle, melt the butter, add the salt pork and fry gently until it starts to brown. Add the celery and onion, and cook 1 minute. Add the potatoes, water, bay leaf and seasoning, bring to a boil, cover and simmer 10–15 minutes or until potatoes are almost tender. Take pan from heat.

Mix a little milk into the flour to make a smooth paste; stir into the soup. Add the remaining milk and corn, bring soup to a boil, cover and simmer 10–15 minutes or until the corn is tender. Remove bay leaf, taste for seasoning, sprinkle with chopped parsley and serve with sippets or cheese croûtes.

Fish Chowder

1 lb haddock fillet
1 onion, thinly sliced
2–3 stalks of celery, thinly
   sliced
1 large carrot, thinly sliced
2 tablespoons butter
3 medium potatoes, peeled
   and diced
4 cups fish stock or water
1 teaspoon salt
pepper
¾ cup milk
1 tablespoon chopped parsley
   (for garnish)

Method
Cook the onion, celery and carrot in the butter for 3–4 minutes. Add the potatoes, mix well, and pour in the fish stock or water; season to taste.

Bring the mixture to a boil, simmer 4–5 minutes, then add the fish, cut into small pieces. Cover and simmer for about 15 minutes or until the vegetables are tender. Add the milk, reheat, taste for seasoning, sprinkle with parsley and serve.

Some of the ingredients for chicken and mushroom broth, a delicious homey soup

Chicken and Mushroom Broth

4–5 lb fowl
2 onions, quartered
2 carrots, quartered
2 stalks of celery, sliced
bouquet garni
10 peppercorns
salt

For garnish
$\frac{1}{4}$ lb mushrooms, very thinly
  sliced
$\frac{1}{2}$ tablespoon butter
squeeze of lemon juice

Traditionally this soup was a way of using tough old fowls that otherwise would have been inedible. Only the breast was eaten, but with today's less elderly birds, the legs can be saved to devil (see future Volume) or eat cold.

Method
Put the fowl in a kettle with the onions, carrots, celery, bouquet garni, peppercorns, a little salt and water to cover. Cover and simmer 1½–2 hours or until the fowl is tender. Let cool to tepid, take out the fowl and remove the meat from the bones.

Replace the bones in the kettle, cover and simmer 2–3 hours longer. Add more water during cooking if necessary — at the end there should be about 6–8 cups broth. Strain.

To prepare the garnish: in a pan melt the butter and sauté the mushrooms with the lemon juice for 1–2 minutes or until tender.

Cut the breast meat from the chicken in strips and add with the mushrooms to the broth. Reheat and taste for seasoning.

Manhattan Clam Chowder

3 cups canned chopped clams
1½ cups bottled clam juice
$\frac{1}{4}$ lb salt pork, diced
1 onion, chopped
2 tablespoons flour
1½ cups water
3 medium potatoes, diced
5 tomatoes, peeled, seeded
  and chopped or 3 cups
  canned tomatoes, crushed
1 teaspoon thyme
bay leaf
salt and pepper

Method
In a large saucepan fry the pork over low heat, stirring, until soft. Add the onion and continue cooking until brown. Stir in the flour, pour in the clam juice and water and bring to a boil, stirring.

Add the potatoes, tomatoes, thyme, bay leaf and seasoning, cover and simmer 10 minutes or until the potatoes are tender. Add the chopped clams and simmer 5 minutes longer. Discard bay leaf and taste for seasoning.

Note: accompaniments for soups are given on pages 56–57.

The next two recipes are Italian. Minestrone, based on meat stock, can have pieces of bacon or ham added; minestra is made only with vegetables. Both soups can be adapted to use any available vegetables.

Minestra

2 tablespoons oil
2 carrots, sliced
1 onion, sliced
2 stalks of celery, sliced
about 6 cups water
$\frac{1}{2}$ bay leaf
1 leek, cut into coarse strips
  (optional)
salt and pepper
$\frac{1}{2}$ small cauliflower, divided
  into flowerets
2 small potatoes, diced
clove of garlic, crushed
1 tablespoon chopped parsley
$\frac{1}{2}$–$\frac{3}{4}$ cup grated Parmesan
  cheese (for serving)

Method
In a kettle heat the oil, add the carrots, onion and celery and fry until just beginning to brown; shake the pan and stir occasionally.

Pour on the water and add the bay leaf and the leek, if used. Season lightly, cover and simmer 15–20 minutes.

Add the cauliflower and simmer 10 minutes longer. Add the potatoes and cook 10 minutes longer or until the potatoes are almost tender. Add the garlic and parsley and simmer 10 minutes longer. Remove the bay leaf and taste for seasoning.
Watchpoint: this soup should have body, but if it seems very thick in the early stages of cooking, add more water.

Serve grated Parmesan cheese separately.

Minestrone

$\frac{1}{4}$ cup dried kidney beans,
  soaked overnight and
  drained
5–6 cups stock
1 tablespoon oil
2 slices of salt pork, chopped
1–2 cloves of garlic, crushed
6–8 small whole carrots or
  3 medium carrots, sliced
3 stalks of celery, sliced
1 large onion, sliced
2 leeks, sliced (optional)
1 cup canned Italian-style
  plum tomatoes or $\frac{1}{2}$ cup
  tomato purée
bouquet garni
salt and pepper
$\frac{1}{2}$ small cauliflower, divided
  into flowerets
1½ cups shredded cabbage
  ($\frac{1}{4}$ small head)
$\frac{1}{2}$–$\frac{3}{4}$ cup grated Parmesan
  cheese (for serving)

Method
Put the kidney beans in a pan with about 2 cups stock, cover, bring slowly to a boil and simmer 1 hour.

In a kettle heat the oil and fry the salt pork until lightly browned. Add the garlic, carrots, celery and onion and fry about 5 minutes or until golden.

Add remaining stock with the leeks, if used, tomatoes or tomato purée and bouquet garni. Season and add the beans with their stock. Cover and simmer 20 minutes.

Add the cauliflower and cook 10 minutes longer. Add the cabbage and simmer 15 minutes longer or until the vegetables are well cooked and the soup has a good flavor. Discard bouquet garni and taste for seasoning.
Watchpoint: this soup should have body, but if it seems very thick in the early stages of cooking, add more stock.

Serve grated Parmesan cheese separately.

Potage Palestine, made with Jerusalem artichokes, may be served with bread sticks or cheese croissants (see page 57)

CREAM SOUPS

Cream of Carrot Soup

5–6 carrots, sliced
1 onion, finely chopped
3 tablespoons butter
4 cups stock
pinch of sugar
salt and pepper
½ small clove of garlic, crushed
¾ cup half and half
1 teaspoon arrowroot, mixed to a paste with 1 tablespoon water (for liaison) – optional

For garnish
¼ cup boiled rice, or croûtons
2 teaspoons chopped mint

Method
In a kettle melt 2 tablespoons of the butter, add the carrots and onion, cover pan and cook over very low heat for 10 minutes or until the vegetables are beginning to soften but are not brown. Stir in the stock, cover the pan and simmer 30–40 minutes or until the vegetables are soft.

Purée the soup in a blender or work it through a food mill or sieve. Add the sugar and seasoning to taste with the garlic. Add half and half and bring the soup just back to a boil.

If necessary, thicken the soup by stirring in the arrowroot paste liaison and heat, stirring, until the soup just thickens. Take the soup from the heat, whisk in the remaining butter in small pieces and add the cooked rice and chopped mint. If serving croûtons, serve in a separate bowl.

Cream of Potato Soup

3 medium potatoes, finely sliced
1 onion, finely sliced
3 tablespoons butter
1 bay leaf
2½ cups milk
1½ cups water
salt and pepper
croûtons or savory butter (for garnish) – optional

For liaison
1–2 egg yolks
5 tablespoons heavy cream

Method
In a kettle melt the butter, add the potatoes and onion and press a piece of foil on top. Cover with a lid and sweat them (cook very slowly) for 10–12 minutes until tender, but do not let them brown.

Remove the foil, add the bay leaf, milk, water and seasoning, bring to a boil, cover and simmer the soup for 20–25 minutes or until the vegetables are very soft.

Watchpoint: it is important that the onions are thoroughly cooked before the milk is added or it may curdle. This is due to the acid in the onion. The soup may also curdle if boiled instead of simmered.

Remove the bay leaf and purée the soup in a blender or work it through a food mill or sieve. Rinse out the kettle, add the soup, reheat and adjust seasoning.

For the liaison: mix the egg yolks and cream in a bowl, stir in a little hot soup and gradually add this mixture to the remaining hot soup, whisking well. Stir over the heat until very hot and the soup thickens slightly, but do not boil or the liaison will curdle. Serve with croûtons or a savory butter.

Potage Palestine (Cream of Artichoke Soup)

1 lb Jerusalem artichokes
juice of ½ lemon
2 tablespoons butter
2 onions, thinly sliced
4 cups stock
1 clove
¼ teaspoon ground nutmeg
salt and pepper
1 cup milk

For liaison
2 egg yolks
½ cup heavy cream

This soup takes its name because it is made with Jerusalem or root artichokes.

Method
Peel the artichokes and thinly slice them; drop them in water with the lemon juice added to prevent them from browning.

In a kettle melt the butter and add the onion. Dry the artichokes on paper towels, add to the onion, cover and cook very gently for 10–15 minutes, stirring occasionally, until the vegetables are very tender.

Add the stock, spices and seasoning, bring to a boil, cover and simmer 10–15 minutes. Discard the clove and work the soup through a sieve or purée it in a blender. Reheat it with the milk.

To prepare the liaison: in a bowl mix the egg yolks and cream and stir in a little of the hot soup. Add this mixture to the remaining soup and heat gently, stirring, until the soup thickens slightly.

Watchpoint: do not let the soup boil or it will curdle.

Taste the soup for seasoning and serve with cheese croissants (see page 57).

PUREE SOUPS

Tomato and Rice Soup

3–4 large ripe tomatoes
1½ tablespoons rice
1 clove of garlic, crushed
2 bay leaves
3 tablespoons butter
2 onions, finely sliced
2 teaspoons flour
4 cups stock or water
1 teaspoon sugar
salt
black pepper, freshly ground
cheese or mustard croûtes (for garnish) – optional

Method
Scald and peel the tomatoes, cut in quarters, remove the seeds and cut one tomato into neat strips for garnish. Coarsely chop the rest and put in a saucepan with the garlic, bay leaves and 1½ tablespoons of the butter. Cover and cook over very low heat for 15 minutes, remove bay leaves, then purée in a blender or work through a sieve or food mill.

Melt the remaining butter in a kettle, add the onions, cover and cook slowly for 15 minutes or until very soft. Take from heat, stir in the flour and the puréed tomatoes and pour on the stock or water. Bring to a boil, add the sugar, seasoning and rice, cover and simmer 20–30 minutes.

Add the reserved tomato strips just before serving with cheese or mustard croûtes.

Red Bean Soup

1 cup dried red kidney beans, soaked overnight
$\frac{1}{4}$ cup butter
1 onion, sliced
1 carrot, sliced
2 medium tomatoes
2 teaspoons tomato paste
bouquet garni
6–7 cups stock or water
salt and pepper

To serve
$\frac{1}{4}$–$\frac{1}{2}$ cup grated sharp Cheddar cheese
croûtons (for garnish)

This soup can also be served as a broth. To do this, scald and peel the tomatoes and do not purée the soup. Dried red kidney beans can be replaced with either dried navy beans or with brown Dutch beans.

Method
Drain the beans.

Melt the butter in a kettle, add the beans, onion and carrot, cover and cook slowly for about 6 minutes.

Halve the unpeeled tomatoes, remove the seeds and press the seeds in a strainer to remove the juice. Add the tomato flesh and juice to the kettle with the tomato paste, bouquet garni and 6 cups stock or water and season.

Bring the soup very slowly to a boil, cover and simmer gently for about 2 hours or until the beans are very tender. Remove the bouquet garni and purée the soup in a blender or work it through a food mill or sieve. Rinse out the kettle, add soup and reheat.

Add the remaining stock if the soup is too thick and adjust the seasoning. Serve grated cheese and croûtons separately.

Mulligatawny

1 lb piece lean breast of lamb
2 tablespoons oil or butter
2 onions, sliced
1 carrot, sliced
1 small tart apple, cored and sliced
1 tablespoon curry powder
$1\frac{1}{2}$ tablespoons flour
6 cups cold water
$\frac{3}{4}$ cup milk
1 teaspoon lemon juice
salt and pepper

For liaison (optional)
1 teaspoon arrowroot, mixed to a paste with 1 tablespoon water

Mulligatawny soup is one of the many dishes created by the British living in India during the heyday of the British Empire. The soup can be made with any kind of meat or trimmings of meat. Alternatively, stock can be used instead of water and the meat may be omitted.

Method
Melt the oil or butter in a large kettle and brown the meat on all sides. Remove it, add the onions, carrot and apple and cook, stirring occasionally, for 3–4 minutes. Add the curry powder, cook 2 minutes more and stir in the flour. Add the water, bring to a boil and put in the meat. Cover and simmer gently for 1–$1\frac{1}{2}$ hours.

Take out the meat and purée the liquid and vegetables in a blender or work them through a food mill or sieve. If using a blender, also add about half the meat, otherwise discard it.

Rinse out the kettle, add the soup, stir in the milk and bring just to a boil.

Watchpoint: if the soup was not puréed in a blender, it may be thin. If so, stir in the arrow-root paste liaison and cook, stirring, until the soup just thickens.

Take from the heat, stir in lemon juice and taste for seasoning. If you like, a few shreds of cooked meat may be added to soup for garnish.

Shrimp and Rice Soup

1 lb small uncooked shrimps
2 tablespoons rice
6 cups water
$\frac{1}{2}$ lb fish bones
1 onion, chopped
1 carrot, chopped
clove of garlic, crushed
bouquet garni
6 peppercorns
1 teaspoon caraway seeds
2 cups milk
salt and pepper

Method
Simmer the shrimps in the water with a little salt for 2–3 minutes or until they are just tender. Drain and reserve the liquid. Peel the shrimps, reserving the shells, and discarding the black vein along the back.

Return the shells to the cooking liquid with the fish bones, onion, carrot, garlic, bouquet garni, peppercorns and caraway seeds. Cover and simmer 30 minutes. Strain and if necessary reduce by boiling to 4 cups.

Simmer the rice, covered, in the milk for 20 minutes or until very soft, stirring occasionally.

Reserve $\frac{1}{2}$ cup cooked shrimps for garnish and purée the rest with the milk and rice in a blender or work through a sieve. Stir in the fish stock, bring to a boil and taste the soup for seasoning. Garnish each bowl with a few of the reserved shrimps.

TO SERVE WITH SOUPS

Almost all soups are improved by a garnish that adds a contrast of flavor, color and texture. Crisply fried croûtons, or light-as-air miniature cheese puffs go well with cream and purée soups. Sippets (triangles of bread dried in a very low oven) are good with broths. Serve these croûtons, croûtes, sippets and puffs separately.

A circle of savory maître d'hôtel or anchovy butter can be placed on top of a bowl of potato or celery soup just before serving.

The appearance of many soups is improved by a sprinkling of chopped parsley or, where appropriate, of chives. Finely chopped egg white or sieved egg yolk also gives a good contrast of color. Bright colored cream or purée soups, such as pea or tomato, look attractive when a spoonful of cream is added to each bowl, then swirled slightly to give a marbled effect.

Croûtons

2–3 slices of dry white bread, crusts removed
2–3 tablespoons oil
2–3 tablespoons butter

Method
Cut the bread into small cubes. In a small frying pan heat the oil and butter and add the bread — the fat should be deep enough to cover the cubes. Fry the croûtons briskly for about 30 seconds, turning them so they brown evenly. Lift them out with a slotted spoon or pour them into a

wire strainer with a bowl beneath to catch the fat.

Spread the croûtons on paper towels to drain thoroughly and sprinkle them with a little salt just before serving.

If you like, fry the croûtons in advance and reheat them 1–2 minutes in a hot oven (400°F).

Serve separately with cream or purée soups.

Potato Croûtons

2 medium potatoes
$\frac{1}{4}$ cup oil
$\frac{1}{4}$ cup butter

Method
Cook the potatoes, unpeeled, in boiling salted water for 10 minutes or until almost tender. Drain and peel while hot; cut into cubes. Fry, drain and serve like bread croûtons.

They are especially good with spinach, tomato or celery soup.

Mustard Croûtes

2 slices of white bread
2 tablespoons grated Cheddar cheese
1 tablespoon butter
$\frac{1}{2}$ teaspoon Dijon-style mustard

Method
Toast bread on one side only. Mix cheese, butter and mustard and spread on untoasted side of bread. Brown under broiler and cut into strips.

Serve mustard croûtes hot with purée soups.

Cheese Croûtes

Leftover cream, cheese, or onion sauces make good croûtes. Toast bread on one side, spread the untoasted side with sauce and sprinkle with grated Cheddar cheese. Brown under the broiler, then cut into strips.

Serve cheese croûtes hot with broths and purée soups.

Sippets

Cut very thin slices of white bread diagonally to make 4 triangles. Lay them on a baking sheet with another sheet on top to prevent the slices from curling; bake in a very low oven (below 200°F) until dry and crisp. They should be cream-colored and not as dark as Melba toast.

Cheese Croissants

1 package prepared dough for crescent rolls
$\frac{1}{2}$ cup grated Parmesan cheese
1 egg, beaten to mix with
$\frac{1}{2}$ teaspoon salt (for glaze)

Makes 8 crescents.

Method
Set the oven at moderately hot (375°F).

Unroll the crescent dough, brush with egg glaze and sprinkle with the grated cheese, reserving 2 tablespoons. Divide the dough into triangles, roll up with the right angle corner to the outside. Curve into crescents and set them on a greased baking sheet.

Brush the crescent with the egg glaze, sprinkle with the

remaining grated cheese and bake in the heated oven for 10–12 minutes or until the crescents are golden brown.

Choux Puffs

If possible, use a little choux pastry left from a large batch made for some other purpose. If necessary, make a small amount of pastry in the following proportions (be sure to measure very accurately):

For choux pastry: $\frac{1}{4}$ cup flour, pinch of salt, $\frac{1}{4}$ cup water, 2 tablespoons butter, 1 egg.

Make the pastry dough (see page 78) and spoon it into a pastry bag fitted with a $\frac{1}{4}$ inch plain tube; pipe tiny mounds on a dampened baking sheet. Bake in a hot oven (400°F) for 12–15 minutes or until the puffs are brown and crisp. Cool and use within a few hours if possible as the puffs toughen on standing.

Cheese Puffs

Follow the recipe for choux puffs and add 2 tablespoons grated Parmesan cheese to the dough before piping.

Savory Butters

Any of the savory butters suggested as broiling accompaniments in Volume 3 go well with mild purée soups like potato. Add a pat to each bowl just before serving.

Cheese Butter

Cream 2 tablespoons butter and beat in 2 tablespoons grated Parmesan or sharp Cheddar cheese with some ground white pepper and a little salt. Shape into a cylinder, roll in wax paper, chill and cut into circles, or spread flat on wax paper, chill and cut into squares.

HOW TO MAKE SPONGE CAKES

Sponges are the lightest of all cakes. They are based on eggs and sugar, beaten until light and fluffy before folding in a small proportion of flour. The texture of the cake depends almost entirely on the amount of air beaten into the eggs, as other leavening agents are rarely added. The mixture is delicate and it is important that there should be no delays in mixing and baking. As always, preparation plays a big part in the success of the finished cake and it is essential to beat the eggs thoroughly. Angel cake (a recipe was given in Volume 1) is made only with the whites of eggs, sugar and cake flour, and is the lightest of all sponge cakes.

Many sponge cakes contain no fat but the continental-type mixture called Génoise has butter added for richness — this will be discussed in a future Volume.

With the exception of Génoise, sponge cakes and jelly rolls are best when eaten very fresh, although they can be stored in an airtight tin for a few days.

General Preparation

Ingredients

All-purpose or cake flour may be used, depending on the recipe. Unless otherwise specified use all-purpose flour for the recipes in this Volume. Sift cake flour 2–3 times and sift even more if using all-purpose flour.

Eggs must be at room temperature to give the greatest volume.

Granulated sugar is most often used for sponge cakes but occasionally a recipe calls for sugar syrup or sugar cubes.

Mixing

Be sure that the bowl and whisk are free of grease so that the eggs rise to the fullest extent.

If beating by hand, use a rotary beater and a deep bowl, or a balloon whisk and a more rounded bowl. Set the bowl over a pan of hot water to get the greatest volume from the eggs and to help the sugar dissolve. If using an electric beater, heat is not necessary.

The egg and sugar mixture is ready when a little lifted on the whisk or beater falls in a thick ribbon on the rest of the mixture and holds its shape. The mixture should be smooth, fluffy and light in color. Take care not to lose any of the air from this mixture when adding the flour. Remove the whisk or beater, sift one-third of the flour over the surface of the batter and cut and fold it in with a metal spoon. When almost mixed, sift one-third more flour over and continue until all the flour is added and the mixture is just smooth. Stop folding as soon as this point is reached. Pour the batter at once into the prepared pans and bake the cake immediately.

Cake Pans

American-style sponge cakes do not have a sugary coating. The pans are not prepared in any way so the mixture clings to the sides of the pan as it rises. Cakes must be left in the pan to cool completely before turning out.

All European-style sponge cakes should be cooled for 1–2 minutes in the pan, then turned out on a wire rack to finish cooling.

Here we use the European method of preparing cake pans for sponge cakes.

For sponge cakes to have a firm, sugary coating in the European style, brush or rub the pans with a little melted or creamed shortening and be sure to reach the corners. Pour a little granulated sugar into the pan, shake it well to coat the base and sides and tip out the excess. Tap the pan to remove any surplus, then repeat the process with a little sifted flour.

Oven Temperatures

Heat oven to the correct temperature at least 20 minutes before baking. Most sponge mixtures are baked in a moderate (350°F) or moderately hot (375°F) oven. Arrange the shelves so that the cake will be in the center of the oven – this ensures constant heat and even baking.

Be sure to use the right size pan as sponge cakes baked in too large or too small a pan will not rise properly. Also, baking times will be different from those indicated in the recipe.

Tests for baking

Sponge mixtures should be baked until delicately golden, not dark brown. When done, a cake starts shrinking from the sides of the pan and the top springs back when lightly pressed with a fingertip.

Sponge Cake 1

¾ cup flour
pinch of salt
3 eggs
½ cup sugar

8 inch springform pan

This soft sponge cake is good for filling with cream and serving with fruit.

Method

Set oven at moderately hot (375°F). Grease the cake pan and sprinkle with sugar and flour, discarding the excess.

Sift the flour and salt 3–4 times. Put eggs in a bowl and gradually beat in the sugar.

If using an electric beater, continue beating at medium speed until the mixture is thick and fluffy – this will take at least 8–10 minutes and the mixture will increase in volume and lighten in color. When dropped from the beater it will make a ribbon trail on the rest of the mixture.

If beating by hand, have a pan of boiling water ready. Beat the sugar into the eggs, then place the bowl over the pan of boiling water, off the heat, and beat for at least 5 minutes until the mixture leaves a ribbon trail. The mixing bowl should rest firmly on the pan without touching the water. Remove bowl from the pan and continue beating until the mixture is cold.

With a metal spoon, cut and fold the flour into the mixture. Pour batter into the prepared pan and bake in heated oven for 20–25 minutes until the cake is golden and the top springs back when lightly pressed with a fingertip. Turn out onto a wire rack to cool.

Sponge Cake 2

¾ cup cake flour
pinch of salt
3 eggs
¾ cup sugar

9 inch tube pan, or 8 inch springform pan

This firm, dry cake is best soaked with fruit juice, or can be filled with a butter cream frosting.

Method

Set oven at moderately hot (375°F). Grease the cake pan and sprinkle with sugar and flour, discarding the excess.

Prepare cake batter as for sponge cake 1. Bake in heated oven for 25–30 minutes until the cake is golden and the top springs back when lightly pressed with a fingertip. Turn out onto a wire rack to cool.

Sponge Cake 3

1 cup flour
pinch of salt
2 eggs
2 egg yolks
½ lb cube sugar
¾ cup water
grated rind of 1 lemon

9 inch springform pan

This cake is excellent for coating with frosting as it is firm and smooth when baked.

Method

Set oven at moderate (350°F). Grease the cake pan and sprinkle with sugar and flour, discarding the excess.

Sift the flour and salt several times. Beat eggs and egg yolks in a bowl until well mixed. In a saucepan dissolve sugar cubes in the water over gentle heat, then boil steadily until the syrup spins a short thread between the finger and thumb (234°F on a sugar thermometer). Gradually pour the boiling syrup into the eggs, beating constantly, and continue beating 8-10 minutes or until the mixture forms a ribbon trail on itself — it should be quite cool. Beat in the lemon rind.

With a metal spoon cut and fold the flour into the egg mixture. Pour batter into prepared pan and bake in heated oven for 45–55 minutes or until the cake top springs back when lightly pressed with a fingertip. Lower the heat to moderately low (325°F) after 30 minutes if the cake is browning too much. Turn out onto a wire rack to cool.

A crusty top sponge cake is surrounded by sponge pennies and ladyfingers

Crusty Top Sponge Cake

1 cup flour
pinch of salt
4 eggs, separated
1 cup sugar
2 teaspoons orange flower
    water

8 inch springform pan

Method
Set oven at moderate (350°F). Grease the pan and sprinkle with sugar and flour, discarding the excess.

Sift the flour and salt together several times. Mix the egg yolks with half the sugar and the orange flower water in a bowl and beat with an electric beater, heavy whisk or flat wooden spoon until the mixture is very thick and light colored.

Beat the egg whites until they hold a stiff peak and beat in the remaining sugar, a tablespoon at a time, until the mixture holds a stiff peak again. With a metal spoon fold the egg white mixture into the yolk mixture alternately with the flour.

Pour the batter into the prepared pan and bake in heated oven for about 45 minutes or until the cake top springs back when lightly pressed with a fingertip. Turn out onto a wire rack to cool.

Ladyfingers

⅓ cup flour
pinch of salt
2 eggs, separated
1 extra egg white
⅓ cup confectioners' sugar, sifted
½ teaspoon vanilla
confectioners' sugar (for sprinkling)

Pastry bag and ½ inch plain tube

Makes 14–16 ladyfingers.

Method

Set oven at low (300°F).

Cover a baking sheet with silicone paper, or grease it and coat lightly with flour.

Sift the flour and salt together several times. Beat egg yolks with an electric or rotary beater until very thick and pale in color. Beat egg whites until they hold a stiff peak, then gradually beat in the sugar to make a thick shiny meringue. Add vanilla to yolks and beat thoroughly, then fold in meringue. Sift all the flour on top and fold in with a large metal spoon.

Spoon this batter carefully into the pastry bag fitted with a plain tube and pipe fingers about 3½ inches long and 1 inch apart on the prepared sheet. Sprinkle the tops with confectioners' sugar and bake in heated oven for 18-20 minutes or until pale beige in color. Remove the ladyfingers immediately from the baking sheet and cool on a wire rack.

Biscuit Milanaise

½ cup cake flour
½ cup potato starch or arrowroot
pinch of salt
4 eggs, 2 of them separated
1 cup sugar
grated rind of 1 lemon
¼ cup currants

8 inch springform pan

Method

Set the oven at moderate (350°F). Grease the pan and sprinkle with sugar and flour, discarding the excess.

Sift flour and potato starch or arrowroot with the salt several times. Put 2 eggs and 2 egg yolks into a bowl and gradually beat in the sugar. If beating by hand set the bowl over a pan of hot water. If using an electric beater no heat is necessary. Beat 5–10 minutes or until the mixture falls from the beater in a ribbon. If beating by hand, take from the heat and beat until cool.

Beat the egg whites until they hold a stiff peak and, with a metal spoon, fold into the egg and sugar mixture alternately with the sifted flour and potato starch mixture, lemon rind and currants.

Pour into prepared pan and bake in heated oven for about 40–50 minutes or until the cake top springs back when lightly pressed with a fingertip. Lower the heat to moderately hot (325°F) after 30 minutes if the cake is browning too much. Turn out onto a wire rack to cool.

Sponge Pennies

⅓ cup cake flour
pinch of salt
3 eggs, separated
6 tablespoons sugar
1 teaspoon orange flower water or lemon juice
confectioners' sugar (for sprinkling)

Pastry bag and ½ inch plain tube (optional)

Makes about 36 'pennies'.

Method

Set oven at moderately low (325°F) and grease and flour a baking sheet.

Sift the flour and salt together several times. Put the egg yolks in a bowl and gradually beat in the sugar with an electric beater, whisk or a flat wooden spoon. Continue beating until the mixture is very thick and light colored. Beat in orange flower water or lemon juice.

Beat the egg whites until they hold a stiff peak, fold one-quarter of them into the yolk mixture, then fold in the flour with a metal spoon. Carefully cut and fold the remaining egg white into the mixture.

Fill the pastry bag fitted with a plain tube with the mixture and pipe rounds (or shape them with a teaspoon) about 1½ inches in diameter onto the baking sheet. Sprinkle generously with confectioners' sugar and bake in heated oven for 15–20 minutes or until lightly browned. Transfer to a wire rack to cool.

Sponge Cupcakes

½ cup flour
pinch of salt
3 eggs
6 tablespoons sugar
extra sugar (for sprinkling)

10–12 muffin pans; 10–12 paper baking cups

Method

Set oven at moderate (350°F). Place baking cups inside muffin pans.

Make batter as for sponge cake 1 (see page 60) and pour into the baking cups to half fill them. Sprinkle the tops with sugar and bake in heated oven for about 20 minutes or until the tops spring back when lightly pressed with a fingertip. Take from the pans and cool.

Flavorings for Sponge Cakes

Orange flower water, the traditional flavoring for sponge cake mixtures, is available in specialty markets and pharmacies.

Grated lemon or orange rind can be used as an alternative, but do not overdo it. The grated rind of a small orange or lemon is quite enough for a 3-egg cake; too much will make the cake sticky.

Another interesting alternative is to place 2-3 leaves of sweet (rose) geranium or lemon verbena leaves on the bottom of the prepared cake pan before pouring in the mixture. This gives a delicate flavor to a plain sponge cake.

Orange Sponge Cake

grated rind of 1 orange
¼ cup orange juice
1½ cups flour
3 eggs
¾ cup sugar
¼ teaspoon almond extract
confectioners' sugar (for
    sprinkling), or orange frosting

Medium loaf pan (8½ X 4½ X 2½ inches)

Method

Set oven at moderate (350°F). Grease the loaf pan and sprinkle with sugar and flour, discarding the excess.

Sift the flour several times. Beat the eggs until mixed and gradually beat in the sugar. Set the bowl over a pan of hot water, off the heat, and continue beating until the mixture is light and leaves a ribbon trail when the whisk is lifted. Take from the heat and continue beating until the mixture is cool. If using an electric beater, no heat is necessary.

Beat in the orange rind and juice, with the almond extract, a little at a time. Fold in the flour in three batches, using a metal spoon. Spoon the batter into the prepared pan and bake in the heated oven for 40–50 minutes or until the top of the cake springs back when lightly pressed with a fingertip.

Turn out onto a wire rack to cool and sprinkle with confectioners' sugar before serving, or cover the top of the cake with orange frosting.

Orange Frosting

1–2 tablespoons orange juice
grated rind of 1 orange
¼ cup butter
2 cups confectioners' sugar

Method

In a pan melt the butter, take from the heat and beat in the confectioners' sugar and the orange rind, with enough orange juice to make a stiff mixture.

Gâteau aux Fruits
(Sponge Cake with Fruits)

1 pint fresh strawberries, halved, or 1 cup black or green grapes, halved and seeded
1 orange, sectioned
1 banana, cut in diagonal slices
¾ cup canned pineapple chunks, drained, or 1 fresh peach, peeled, pitted and sliced, or ¾ cup canned peach slices, drained
1–2 tablespoons apricot jam
¼ cup slivered almonds

For syrup
½ cup sugar
1 cup water
1 tablespoon rum or kirsch or 1 teaspoon vanilla

For sponge cake
½ cup cake flour
pinch of salt
2 eggs
½ cup sugar

Ring mold (5–6 cup capacity)

Method

To make the syrup: heat the sugar with the water until dissolved, bring to a boil and simmer 5 minutes. Let cool, add the prepared fruit with the rum or kirsch and vanilla, cover and chill 3–4 hours.

Set the oven at moderately hot (375°F). Grease the ring mold and sprinkle it with sugar and flour, discarding the excess.

Sift the flour and salt 3–4 times. Put the eggs in a bowl and gradually beat in the sugar. Set the bowl over a pan of hot water, off the heat, and beat until the mixture is light and leaves a ribbon trail when the beater is lifted. Take from the heat and continue beating until the mixture is cool. If using an electric beater, no heat is necessary.

Pour the batter into the prepared mold and bake in the heated oven for 20–25 minutes or until the top of the cake springs back when lightly pressed with a fingertip. Turn out onto a wire rack to cool.

Set the cake on a platter and spoon about ½ cup syrup from the fruit over it. Pile the fruit in the center and around the cake.

In a saucepan melt the apricot jam with about ¼ cup of the remaining fruit syrup and spoon over the cake to glaze it. Sprinkle the cake with slivered almonds.

Almond Angel Cake

½ cup shredded almonds
¾ cup cake flour
1¼ cups sugar
1 cup egg whites (about 6 large eggs)
¼ teaspoon salt
1 teaspoon cream of tartar
½ teaspoon almond extract
confectioners' sugar (for sprinkling)

8 inch springform pan

Method

Set the oven at moderate (350°F).

Sift the flour 3 times with ¾ cup of the sugar. In a large bowl, beat the egg whites with the salt until foamy. Add the cream of tartar and beat until the egg whites stand in a stiff peak. Add the remaining sugar, 2 tablespoons at a time, beating between each addition until glossy. Add the almond extract with the last portion of sugar.

Sift the flour and sugar mixture over the egg whites, ¼ cup at a time; fold in lightly with a metal spoon. Gently spoon the mixture into the ungreased pan, level the surface and draw a knife through the mixture to break any air bubbles. Sprinkle the shredded almonds on top of the batter and bake in heated oven for 40–45 minutes or until the top of the cake springs back when lightly pressed with a fingertip.

Invert the pan over a wire rack to cool, making sure that the top of the cake does not touch the rack. When cold, loosen the sides of the cake with a spatula and remove the pan sides, then loosen the base. Sprinkle the cake with confectioners' sugar before serving.

Almond angel cake, topped with browned shredded almonds, is sprinkled with confectioners' sugar

Timbale Orta may be served hot or cold with sabayon sauce poured over

Timbale Orta

For sponge cake
1 cup self-rising flour
pinch of salt
$\frac{1}{2}$ cup butter
$\frac{1}{3}$ cup sugar
grated rind and juice of $\frac{1}{2}$ small
    orange
2 eggs, beaten to mix

For cherry compote
1$\frac{1}{2}$ lb fresh tart red cherries,
    pitted, or 2 cans (16 oz and
    8 oz each) pitted tart red
    cherries, drained
$\frac{1}{2}$ cup sugar (or to taste)
$\frac{1}{4}$ teaspoon ground cinnamon
2 tablespoons brandy
1–2 tablespoons red currant
    jelly

*Charlotte mold (4–5 cup
  capacity)*

Method
Set oven at moderate (350°F). Grease the mold and sprinkle with flour, discarding the excess.

To make the cake: sift the flour with the salt. In a bowl cream the butter, beat in the sugar and orange rind and continue beating until the mixture is light and soft. Add the eggs, a little at a time, beating thoroughly between each addition. Using a metal spoon, fold in the flour alternately with the orange juice.

Spoon the cake batter into the prepared mold and bake in the heated oven for about 45 minutes or until the top of the cake springs back when lightly pressed with a finger-tip. Loosen the edge of the cake with a spatula and turn out onto a wire rack to cool.

To make the compote: place the fresh cherries in a saucepan with the sugar and cinnamon. Cover and cook gently, shaking the pan occasionally, until the juice

runs. If using canned cherries, combine with the sugar and cinnamon in a pan, but do not cook.

Add the brandy to the fresh or canned cherries, cover and cook 10–15 minutes longer or until the cherries are very tender. Stir in the red currant jelly with more sugar if needed to taste.

Turn over the cake and hollow out the underside. Fill with the hot cherry compote and cover with a lid made from the cut out piece of cake. Turn the cake right way up onto a platter. Spoon sabayon sauce over the top and serve the rest separately. Serve hot sabayon sauce if the timbale is hot, or cold sabayon sauce if the timbale is cold.

Spoon the hot cinnamon and brandy-flavored cherry compote into the hollowed-out sponge cake

Hot Sabayon Sauce

3 egg yolks
1 tablespoon sugar
$\frac{1}{2}$ cup sherry
small strip of lemon rind

Makes about 1–1$\frac{1}{2}$ cups.

Method
Combine all the ingredients in the top of a double boiler and whisk over hot but not boiling water until the mixture is very frothy and slightly thick. Remove the lemon rind and serve at once.

Cold Sabayon Sauce

$\frac{1}{4}$ cup sugar
$\frac{1}{4}$ cup water
2 egg yolks
grated rind and juice of $\frac{1}{2}$ lemon
1 tablespoon rum or brandy,
    or 2 tablespoons sherry
$\frac{3}{4}$ cup heavy cream, whipped
    until it holds a soft shape

Makes about 1–1$\frac{1}{2}$ cups.

Method
Dissolve the sugar in the water over gentle heat, then boil the syrup until it spins a thread between your finger and thumb when a little is lifted on a spoon (230°F–234°F on a sugar thermometer).

Beat the egg yolks well, take the syrup from the heat and as soon as the bubbles have subsided, pour it gradually onto the egg yolks, beating constantly. Continue beating until the mixture is very thick.

Beat in the lemon rind and juice. Flavor with rum, brandy or sherry and continue to beat 1–2 minutes or until cool. Fold the whipped cream into the mixture and chill.

For hot sabayon sauce, whisk the egg yolk mixture over hot water until it is frothy and slightly thick

Jelly Roll 1

¾ cup flour
¾ teaspoon baking powder
pinch of salt
3 eggs
¾ cup sugar
3 tablespoons water
½ teaspoon vanilla
granulated or confectioners'
   sugar (for sprinkling)

For filling
½ cup any kind of jam, melted

Jelly roll pan, or paper case
* 10 X 15 inches*

This jelly roll recipe is easier to make than the second one, but do not overbake the mixture or it will crack when rolled.

Method
Set oven at moderately hot (375°F). Grease and flour the jelly roll pan or paper case if using wax paper.

Sift the flour several times with the baking powder and salt. Beat the eggs until thick, gradually beat in the sugar and continue beating until the mixture is light and makes a ribbon trail.

Stir in the water and vanilla, sprinkle the flour on the mixture all at once and beat until just smooth. Pour into the prepared pan or paper case, spread the batter evenly and bake in heated oven for 12–15 minutes, or until the roll is lightly browned around the edges but still pale, though firm to the touch in the center.

Turn out the cake, trim it, spread with jam and roll up. Just before serving, sprinkle generously with sugar.

How to make a Jelly Roll Case

Take a piece of wax or silicone paper 1–2 inches larger than the size of cake you want to bake — 10 X 15 inches is a common size.

Fold over the ends and sides of the paper to form a border of about 1½ inches and cut a slit at each corner. Fold one cut piece over the other to 'miter' the corner and fasten with a paper clip so the borders stand up. Slide the case onto a baking sheet.

This case can be used for a jelly roll or for the savory roulades that will be described in a future Volume.

Turning out a Jelly Roll

1 *First loosen edges of the cake; turn out immediately onto a clean dish towel or a sheet of wax paper sprinkled with granulated or confectioners' sugar. Then tear paper case away quickly but carefully from jelly roll*

2 *Trim sides of jelly roll with a knife to make a neat edge and to remove the brown crust*

3 *Spread jelly roll with warm jam; roll up at once by gently tilting paper or towel. If not using jam as a filling, roll the towel in with the cake to prevent it from sticking. Leave jelly roll to cool, still wrapped so it does not unroll*

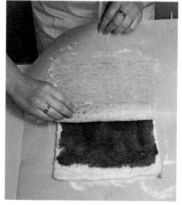

1

2

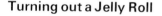
3

Jelly Roll 2

¾ cup flour
1 tablespoon cornstarch
¾ teaspoon baking powder
pinch of salt
¾ cup sugar
3 eggs, separated
1 tablespoon orange flower
   water
granulated or confectioners'
   sugar (for sprinkling)

For filling
½ cup any kind of jam, melted

Jelly roll pan, or paper case
* 10 X 15 inches*

Method
Set oven at moderate (350°F); grease and flour the jelly roll pan or paper case if using wax paper.

Sift the flour 4 times with the cornstarch, baking powder and salt. Set aside 2 tablespoons sugar to add to the egg whites. Beat the egg yolks until thick, beat in about three-quarters of the sugar, then gradually add the remaining sugar with the orange flower water and continue beating until the mixture is thick and light colored and makes a ribbon trail.

Beat the egg whites until they hold a stiff peak, add the 2 tablespoons reserved sugar and continue beating until the mixture stands in a peak again. Fold the egg whites into the yolks and finally fold in the flour with a metal spoon. Pour the batter into the prepared pan or paper case, spread it evenly and bake in heated oven for about 12 minutes or until brown around the edges but still pale in the center.

Turn out the cake, trim it, spread with jam and roll up. Just before serving, sprinkle generously with sugar.

Strawberry or Banana Cream Roll

jelly roll (baked as for recipe 2)
confectioners' sugar
(for sprinkling)

For filling
1 pint ripe strawberries, or
2-3 bananas
$\frac{1}{2}$ teaspoon vanilla
2 cups Chantilly cream

*Jelly roll pan, or paper case
10 X 15 inches*

Method
Make jelly roll and roll it without the filling with paper or a towel inside to prevent it from sticking.

Hull and slice the strawberries or peel and slice bananas. Unroll the cake and spread with the Chantilly cream. Sprinkle with strawberries or bananas and roll up again.

Chill before serving and sprinkle with confectioners' sugar.

Chocolate Roll

1 tablespoon cocoa
6 tablespoons flour
pinch of salt
4 eggs, separated
$\frac{1}{4}$ teaspoon cream of tartar
$\frac{3}{4}$ cup sugar
$\frac{1}{2}$ teaspoon vanilla
confectioners' sugar
(for sprinkling)

For filling
2 cups Chantilly cream,
coffee butter cream frosting,
or cherry filling

*Jelly roll pan, or paper case
10 X 15 inches*

Method
Set oven at moderately hot (325°F); grease and flour the jelly roll pan or paper case if using wax paper.

Sift the flour several times with the cocoa and salt. Beat the egg whites with the cream of tartar until they hold a stiff peak, then gradually beat in half the sugar. Continue beating until the mixture is very glossy and holds a peak again.

Beat the egg yolks until thick, then gradually beat in the remaining sugar with the vanilla. Continue beating until the mixture is thick and light colored. With a metal spoon carefully fold the flour into the egg yolk mixture alternately with the egg whites until well blended.

Pour the batter into the prepared pan or paper case, spread evenly and bake in heated oven for 20–25 minutes or until lightly brown at the edges but still pale at the center. Turn out, trim the edges, and roll up with paper or a towel inside to prevent it from sticking.

When cool, unroll the cake carefully and fill with the Chantilly cream, coffee butter cream frosting or cherry filling. Roll up again and sprinkle with confectioners' sugar before serving.

Chantilly Cream

Whip 1 cup heavy cream until it starts to thicken; add 1 tablespoon sugar and $\frac{1}{2}$ teaspoon vanilla; continue beating until the cream holds a shape. (If the kitchen is warm and the sugar and vanilla are added before the first beating, the cream will not thicken. In very hot weather, chill the cream, bowl and beater before whipping.

Coffee Butter Cream Frosting

2–3 teaspoons dry instant coffee
1 cup unsalted butter
3 egg yolks
6 tablespoons sugar
6 tablespoons water

Method
In a bowl beat the egg yolks lightly until mixed. Dissolve the sugar in the water, bring to a boil and boil until the syrup spins a thread when a little is lifted on a spoon (230°F–234°F on a sugar thermometer). Pour the hot syrup onto the egg yolks, beating hard, and continue beating until the mixture is cool and thick and light. Cream the butter and gradually beat it into the egg and sugar mixture with the instant coffee.

Cherry Filling

1 jar (12 oz) dark cherry jam
1 cup heavy cream, whipped
until it holds a soft shape

Method
In a small pan heat the jam until melted. Strain off the syrup and cool it, reserving the cherries. Beat the cooled syrup into the lightly whipped cream and continue beating until the mixture is stiff. Fold in the cherries.

Plum compote is served with rich almond cake (recipe is on page 75)

POACH PLUMS IN RED WINE FOR A SPECIAL DESSERT

The unusual fruit sauce for the loin of lamb Doria calls for unorthodox suggestions in the way of wine. Red Loire wines are still relatively unknown in this country, but they are available in the major urban areas and their fresh, fruity qualities seem ideally suited to this dish. The cabernet franc grape from which they are made is rarely grown in America, but a related grape, the ruby cabernet, produces a varietal wine that will also go very well with the lamb. Both the Loire and the California wines are best chilled for about 15 minutes before serving.

Cod Cubat

Loin of Lamb Doria
with Orange & Red Currant Sauce
Potatoes Anna

Plum Compote
with Rich Almond Cake

Red wine – Bourgueil (Loire)
or Ruby Cabernet (California)

TIMETABLE

Day before
Make the plum compote, cover securely and refrigerate. Make the almond cake and keep in airtight container.

Morning
Prepare the fish (include crumbs in cheese topping) and place in ovenproof serving dish ready for reheating. Prepare croûtes; drain and cool on paper towels.

Make orange and red currant sauce and set aside in serving bowl.

Peel and cut cucumber; trim scallions. Blanch both these vegetables, refresh and put in pan or casserole with butter and seasonings and let stand until cooking time.

Peel potatoes but leave them whole; cover with cold water.

Brown the chine bone and make stock for gravy.

Assemble equipment for final cooking from 6:15 p.m. for dinner around 8 p.m.

> You will find that **cooking times** given in the individual recipes for these dishes have sometimes been adapted in the timetable to help you when cooking and serving them as a party meal.

Order of Work

6:15
Set oven at hot (400°F).
Transfer plum compote and almond cake to serving dishes.

6:30
Put the lamb in oven and baste frequently.
Dry the potatoes with paper towels and butter the pan for potatoes; slice and arrange them in pan; cover with foil and a plate to weigh them down.

7:00
Turn and baste the lamb.

7:15
Put potatoes over moderate heat for 15 minutes. Baste meat. Put potatoes in oven.

7:30
Lower oven to moderate (350°F).
Put fish in oven to reheat.

7:45
Cook cucumber and scallions.
Put the lamb on an ovenproof platter and return to oven. Drain fat from roasting pan, make gravy, strain and keep hot. Put the croûtes for the fish on rack in oven to heat.
Carve lamb and arrange on platter. Turn out potatoes.
If fish is not lightly browned, broil for about 1 minute.
Arrange croûtes on dish with fish just before serving.

8:00
Serve appetizer.
Reheat cucumber garnish for lamb just before serving.

Appetizer

Cod Cubat

1½ lb cod fillets
salt and pepper
juice of ½ small lemon
2 cups (½ lb) mushrooms, finely chopped
1 tablespoon butter
2 teaspoons chopped mixed herbs
pinch of ground mace

For thick béchamel sauce
2 tablespoons butter
2 tablespoons flour
¾ cup milk (infused with 3 peppercorns, ½ bay leaf, 1 blade of mace)

For mornay sauce
1½ tablespoons butter
1½ tablespoons flour
1¼ cups milk
½ cup grated cheese (Cheddar or half Parmesan and half Gruyère)

To finish
1 tablespoon grated Parmesan cheese
1 dinner roll (for croûtes)
¼ cup oil and butter, mixed (for frying croûtes)

Method
Cut cod fillets into 6–8 portions. Place them in a buttered ovenproof dish and sprinkle with salt, pepper and lemon juice. Cover the fish with buttered foil and bake in a moderately low oven (325°F) for 15 minutes or until it flakes easily when tested with a fork. Drain on paper towels.

Prepare béchamel sauce.

Sauté the mushrooms in butter until all the moisture has evaporated. Stir in the herbs and mace, mix with the béchamel sauce, adjust seasoning, and set aside.

To prepare the mornay sauce: melt the butter in a pan, stir in the flour off the heat and pour in the milk. Cook, stirring constantly, until the sauce comes to a boil. Simmer 2 minutes, take from the heat, beat in the ½ cup of grated cheese and season sauce to taste.

Reheat the mushroom mixture and spread down the center or over the base of a heatproof serving dish, arrange the fish on top and coat with the mornay sauce. Sprinkle with the extra grated Parmesan cheese and brown under the broiler just before serving.

Slice the dinner roll into ½ inch diagonal slices for croûtes and fry in oil and butter until golden brown. Drain on paper towels and use to garnish the dish.

Watchpoint: if the dish is to be baked ahead of time and reheated in the oven later in the day, mix a scant tablespoon of browned crumbs with the cheese that is to be sprinkled on top to prevent little pools of fat from forming.

Place pieces of cooked cod on the mushroom mixture before coating with mornay sauce, then sprinkle with grated cheese and brown lightly

Entrée

Loin of Lamb Doria
with Orange and Red Currant Sauce

2–2½ lb loin of lamb, chine bone removed and reserved
1 onion
1 carrot
4 cups water
salt and pepper
bouquet garni
2–3 tablespoons butter or meat drippings
1 large cucumber
2 bunches of scallions
1½ tablespoons butter
1 teaspoon chopped parsley
2 teaspoons flour

Method
Set oven at hot (400°F).

Put the chine bone from the lamb in a roasting pan and roast, without any fat, for 15 minutes or until lightly browned.

To make the stock: transfer the bone to a saucepan, add the onion, carrot, water, salt and pepper and bouquet garni. Bring slowly to a boil, skim the surface well, simmer for about 1 hour and strain.

Heat the butter or drippings in the roasting pan until sizzling, put in the lamb and baste well. Roast in heated oven 1–1¼ hours for slightly pink meat (160°F on a meat thermometer), or 1¼–1½ hours for well done meat (175°F on a meat thermometer). Baste the meat often during cooking and turn over when half cooked.

Peel the cucumber, cut into quarters lengthwise, and cut across in 2 inch pieces. Trim the scallions, leaving about 2 inches of the green tops.

Blanch and refresh the cucumber and scallions in a pan of boiling water for 1 minute and drain well.

Melt the butter in a shallow pan, add the vegetables, season with salt and pepper, cover and cook over a low heat for 5–8 minutes. Shake the pan occasionally and, as soon as the vegetables are tender, remove from the heat and stir in the parsley.

Watchpoint: If the vegetables are prepared ahead of time, let the cucumber and scallions get cold and reheat just before serving. When cucumber is kept hot or overcooks, it becomes very watery.

When the lamb is done, move it to a heated platter. Discard drippings from the roasting pan, leaving all brown sediment. Sprinkle the pan with flour and stir over a low heat until well browned. Pour on the stock made from the chine bone and bring to a boil, stirring frequently. Reduce heat and simmer until the gravy is well reduced. Taste, adjust the seasoning and serve in a warm gravy boat.

Carve the meat and garnish it with the cucumber mixture. Serve the orange and red currant sauce and potatoes Anna separately.

Orange and Red Currant Sauce

In a bowl mix the rind and juice of 1 orange (when grating orange, take care to remove only the outer rind and none of the white pith); add ¼ cup red currant jelly and stir until it is well mixed. If the jelly is very firm, melt it carefully in a saucepan before adding to the rind and juice.

Stir in 1 tablespoon chopped mint and 1 tablespoon white wine vinegar and serve in a small bowl.

Accompaniment to entrée

Potatoes Anna

4–5 medium potatoes
5–6 tablespoons butter
salt and pepper

6 inch heavy frying pan with ovenproof handle

Method
Butter the bottom and sides of a frying pan very generously.

Peel potatoes, slice them in very thin rounds (a mandoline slicer is excellent for this) and arrange the slices in a neat spiral design to cover the bottom of the pan. After two layers are in the pan, season and dot with butter. Continue layering potatoes in the pan, seasoning and buttering every other layer. Spread any remaining butter on a piece of foil and cover the pan securely.

Put an ovenproof plate on top of the foil to press the potatoes down a little and to prevent steam from escaping during cooking. Set the pan on moderate heat and cook potatoes for 15 minutes or until browned on the bottom. To test this, slide a metal spatula down the side of the potato cake and lift it slightly —the odor of browned (noisette) butter is unmistakable.

Transfer pan to a hot oven (400°F) and bake for about 30 minutes or until the potatoes are very tender. Remove from the oven, and discard the foil. Place a warm serving plate on top and invert the frying pan. The potatoes should turn out in a golden brown cake.

Use a mandoline to cut very thin slices for potatoes Anna

Arrange the potato slices in the bottom of a buttered pan

A **mandoline**, excellent for slicing vegetables, is a rectangular piece of wood or metal fitted with a plain or fluted sharp blade that can be adjusted to regulate the thickness of slices.

Roast lamb Doria is garnished with cucumber and scallions. Serve the lamb with potatoes Anna and orange and red currant sauce

Dessert

Plum Compote
with Rich Almond Cake

1½ lb prune or Italian plums
½ cup red wine or port
¼ cup red currant jelly
grated rind and juice of 1 orange

Method
Pour the wine or port into a saucepan large enough to hold the plums and boil until it is reduced by half. Add the red currant jelly and stir until it is melted, then add the orange rind and juice.

Cut the plums in half and remove the pits. Put them, cut side up, in the pan. Cook over high heat until the syrup boils up and over the fruit. Then reduce the heat and simmer gently until the plums are tender. Allow at least 10 minutes for this, even when the fruit is ripe, so the plums absorb the syrup.

Transfer the plums to a bowl to cool. Serve cold with rich almond cake.

Accompaniment to dessert

Rich Almond Cake

½ cup butter
10 tablespoons sugar
3 eggs
⅔ cup whole blanched almonds, ground
6 tablespoons flour
2–3 drops of almond extract
granulated sugar (for sprinkling)

7 inch springform pan

Method
Grease and flour the cake pan and cover the bottom with a circle of wax paper. Set oven at moderate (350°F). Sift the flour onto a sheet of wax paper.

Cream butter in a bowl and beat in the sugar, 1 tablespoon at a time, until the mixture is soft and light. Beat in eggs, one at a time, and add one-third of the ground almonds with each egg. Beat thoroughly. Fold in the flour and almond extract with a metal spoon until the batter is smooth and pour it into the prepared pan.

Bake the cake in heated oven for 35–45 minutes or until a skewer inserted near the center comes out clean. When baked the cake will shrink slightly from the sides of the springform pan.

To remove the cake from the pan, have 2 wire racks ready and put a paper towel or a clean folded dish towel on 1 of the racks. Loosen the sides of the cake with a small metal spatula, and remove the sides of the pan. Place the rack with paper towel or dish towel on top of the cake (the towel should be next to cake) and turn it over. Remove pan and circle of paper from the bottom. Place second rack on top of the cake base and carefully but quickly turn it over again. This prevents markings on the rack from showing on top of the cake. When the cake is cold, sprinkle the top with granulated sugar.

Orange and red wine give flavor to a fresh plum compote ▶

Pile chocolate profiteroles, with Suchard sauce spooned over, in a pyramid to serve (recipe is on page 82)

HOW TO MAKE PASTRY (3) CHOUX

Choux pastry is quite different from any other type of pastry. To make the dough, flour is added to boiling water and butter so the mixture becomes a firm paste, then eggs are beaten in to make the pastry rise and puff so it is hollow in the center when cooked.

The dough is often baked — éclairs and profiteroles are the most familiar sweet pastries made from choux, but there are savory dishes, like gougère, that are excellent for supper.

Choux pastry can also be deep fried to make sweet or savory fritters (beignets soufflés) or it can be poached in water, then coated with sauce to make gnocchi (a recipe will be given in a future Volume).

Points to remember

1 Measure ingredients carefully as a small inaccuracy can prevent choux pastry dough from rising properly.

2 Bring the butter and water just to a boil – prolonged boiling evaporates the water and changes the proportions of the dough.

3 Add the flour all at once, off the heat, and beat only until the mixture is smooth and comes away from the sides of the pan; the dough will not rise if it is overbeaten at this stage.

4 For a particularly crisp pastry use flour with a high gluten content instead of regular flour – high gluten flour is available at some health food stores.

5 The exact amount of egg needed may vary with the flour used. As the eggs are added the mixture will first stiffen slightly, then soften again. It should be glossy and just soft enough to fall from the spoon. If too little egg is added the dough will not rise properly; if too much, the dough will be too soft to shape and will not become crisp when cooked.

6 Beat the flour mixture thoroughly for 1–2 minutes after adding the eggs – if you like, use an electric mixer at slow speed.

7 A dampened baking sheet helps the dough to rise in the oven – hold the sheet under cold running water for a few seconds.

8 Keep the mounds of dough well separated on the baking sheet so there is room for them to puff during baking.

9 Bake the dough in a rising heat. It is normally baked for 10 minutes in a hot oven (400°F), then baking is completed at 425°F. When deep frying, start cooking at 350°F (on a fat thermometer) and turn the heat up to 375°F once the dough is added so the fat gets hotter as the pastry cooks.

10 Be sure the pastry is brown and crisp before taking it from the oven – pale choux pastry will soften and collapse as it cools. If making small pastries like profiteroles, it is wise to test by cooling one before removing the rest from the oven.

11 When baked, poke a small hole in the side of the choux pastry with a skewer or the point of a knife to release steam and keep the pastry crisp as it cools.

12 Baked choux pastry is best eaten within a few hours, as it tends to lose its crispness and toughen on standing.

Fruit Sauces

For soft fruits such as raspberries or strawberries: work the fresh or frozen fruit through a sieve or purée it in a blender and strain to remove the seeds. Beat in confectioners' sugar to taste and, if necessary, thin to a pouring consistency with water.

For cranberries, plums, or blueberries: poach the fruit in sugar syrup before working it through a sieve or puréeing it in a blender.

Basic Choux Pastry

For 3–4 egg quantity
$\frac{2}{3}$ cup flour
$\frac{1}{4}$ teaspoon salt
$\frac{2}{3}$ cup water
$\frac{1}{3}$ cup butter
3–4 eggs

For 4–5 egg quantity
1 cup flour
$\frac{1}{4}$ teaspoon salt
1 cup water
$\frac{1}{2}$ cup butter
4–5 eggs

The amount of choux pastry needed for 4 people depends on each individual recipe.

Method

Sift the flour with the salt onto a piece of wax paper.

Put the water and butter into a fairly large saucepan, bring to a boil and when bubbling, draw the pan from the heat and immediately pour in all the flour. Beat vigorously for a few seconds until the mixture is smooth and pulls away from the sides of the pan to form a ball.

Cool the mixture about 5 minutes, then beat in the eggs one at a time. If the eggs are large, break the last one into a bowl and beat with a fork to mix. Add this slowly to the pastry dough to ensure that it remains firm and keeps its shape – all of this last egg may not be needed, depending on the consistency of the dough.

Beat the dough for 1–2 minutes until it is glossy and very smooth. It is then ready to be piped from a pastry bag fitted with a plain tube or it can be shaped with a spoon for baking or frying.

SWEET CHOUX

Choux à la Crème (Cream Puffs)

3–4 egg quantity choux pastry
about $1\frac{1}{2}$ cups heavy cream, stiffly whipped
1 tablespoon granulated sugar (or to taste)
confectioners' sugar (for sprinkling)

For rich chocolate sauce
1 package (12 oz) semisweet chocolate pieces
2 squares (2 oz) unsweetened chocolate, chopped
pinch of salt
3 tablespoons strong coffee
1 cup heavy cream
2 tablespoons brandy

Pastry bag and $\frac{3}{8}$ inch and small plain tubes (optional)

Choux are usually piped in 1 inch diameter mounds so they swell to $2–2\frac{1}{2}$ inch puffs. However, they may be made much larger – up to $3\frac{1}{2}$–4 inches across. This chocolate sauce is an extra rich one.

Method

Set oven at hot (400°F).

Prepare the choux pastry dough. Pipe into small mounds using a $\frac{3}{8}$ inch plain tube or shape pastry with a teaspoon and set fairly far apart on dampened baking sheets. Bake 10 minutes in the heated oven, then raise temperature to 425°F and continue baking 10–20 minutes. When crisp and firm to the touch, take out, prick the sides to release steam, and cool on a wire rack.

Make a slit in the side of each puff. Beat sugar to taste into the cream and fill the choux puffs, preferably using a pastry bag fitted with a small plain tube.

Arrange the puffs in a pyramid on a serving dish, sprinkling each layer with confectioners' sugar.

To make the rich chocolate sauce: put both kinds of chocolate, salt and coffee in the top of a double boiler. Let the chocolate melt over hot water, then gradually stir in the cream and brandy; stir until smooth.

Serve the hot chocolate sauce in a separate dish, or alternatively serve a fruit sauce (see box on opposite page).

Gâteau Paris-Brest

3–4 egg quantity of choux pastry
$\frac{1}{4}$ cup shredded almonds
2 cup quantity of coffee-flavored pastry cream
confectioners' sugar (for sprinkling)

Pastry bag; 1 inch plain tube and medium star tube

Paris-Brest is the French name for a crown-shaped pastry filled with a cream mixture and sprinkled with almonds.

Method

Set oven at hot (400°F).

Prepare the choux pastry dough and put it into a pastry bag fitted with a 1 inch plain tube. Pipe the dough in an 8–9 inch ring on a dampened baking sheet. Sprinkle the dough with the almonds and bake 10 minutes in the heated oven. Raise the temperature to 425°F and bake 15–20 minutes longer or until the pastry is browned and crisp. Prick the choux ring to release the steam and let cool on a

wire rack.

Make the coffee-flavored pastry cream and chill thoroughly so it is stiff enough to pipe. Put it in a pastry bag fitted with a medium star tube.

Cut the choux pastry ring in half horizontally, and fill the bottom very full with pastry cream. Put on the top so the cream shows at the sides and sprinkle with confectioners' sugar.

Petits Paris-Brest

Follow the recipe for gâteau Paris-Brest and pipe 3 inch rings using a $\frac{1}{2}$ inch plain tube. Omit the almonds from the top of the choux rings and bake as for the large gâteau, allowing about the same length of time.

Let cool on a wire rack, split the rings and fill them with half of the pastry cream; pipe the remaining pastry cream on top. Sprinkle with $\frac{1}{2}$ cup shredded almonds, browned, and top with confectioners' sugar. Makes about 12 gâteaux.

Pastry Cream

For 2 cup quantity
1 egg, separated
1 egg yolk
$\frac{1}{4}$ cup sugar
$1\frac{1}{2}$ tablespoons flour
1 tablespoon cornstarch
$1\frac{1}{2}$ cups milk
2–3 squares (2–3 oz) semisweet chocolate, chopped, or 1–$1\frac{1}{2}$ tablespoons dry instant coffee

Method

Beat the egg yolks with the sugar until thick and light.

Stir in the flour and cornstarch and just enough cold milk to make a smooth paste.

For chocolate flavoring: melt the chocolate in remaining milk, then bring the mixture to a boil and gradually pour onto the egg mixture. Blend, return it to the pan and stir over gentle heat until boiling.

Watchpoint: make sure the pastry cream is smooth before letting it boil. If lumps form as it thickens, take pan from heat and beat until smooth.

Cook the cream for 2 minutes, stirring. If it is too stiff, stir in a little extra milk.

Whip the egg white until it holds a stiff peak and fold in a little of the hot pastry cream. Fold this mixture into remaining hot cream, pour into a bowl, cover and cool.

For coffee flavoring: make as above (omitting the chocolate) and add 1–$1\frac{1}{2}$ tablespoons instant coffee to milk before adding to yolk mixture.

Strawberry Swans

1 pint small strawberries, hulled
3–4 egg quantity of choux pastry
Chantilly cream, made with $1\frac{1}{2}$ cups heavy cream, stiffly whipped and flavored with $1\frac{1}{2}$–2 tablespoons sugar and 1 teaspoon vanilla
$\frac{1}{4}$ cup pistachios, finely chopped (for sprinkling)
candied angelica leaf, cut in a diamond shape (optional)

Pastry bag; $\frac{3}{8}$ inch plain tube and medium star tube

Makes about 12 swans.

Method

Set the oven at hot (400°F).

Prepare the choux pastry

dough. Put it in a pastry bag fitted with a $\frac{3}{8}$ inch plain tube and pipe into mounds, about $2\frac{1}{2}$ inches in diameter, set far apart on dampened baking sheets; reserve a small portion of the dough.

Bake the puffs in the heated oven for 10 minutes, then raise the temperature to 425°F and bake 15–20 minutes longer. When crisp and firm to the touch, take out the puffs and prick them at the sides to release the steam. Cool on a wire rack.

Lower the oven temperature to hot (400°F). Pipe the remaining dough on a dampened baking sheet in 'S' shapes to form the necks of the swans. Bake in the heated oven for 10–12 minutes or until they are brown and crisp; cool on a wire rack.

A short time before serving, halve the strawberries, reserving a few for decoration. Make the Chantilly cream.

Split the choux puffs and fill the bottoms with strawberries. Fill the Chantilly cream into a pastry bag fitted with a medium star tube and cover the strawberries generously with cream. Cut the tops of the puffs in half and set them on the cream to form wings. Insert the necks of the swans, sprinkle them with chopped pistachios and add a 'tail' of a diamond of angelica, if you like. Arrange the swans on a platter and decorate with strawberries.

Mouth-watering éclairs are covered with chocolate and coffee glacé icing

For choux pastry dough, bring the water and butter to a boil, take from heat and immediately pour in the flour

Beat the flour mixture vigorously until the dough is smooth and pulls away from the sides of the pan

After beating the eggs into the cooled flour mixture, pipe the éclairs onto a dampened baking sheet before baking

Eclairs

4–5 egg quantity of choux pastry (see page 78)
2 cups chocolate, or coffee, pastry cream (see page 79), or 2 cups Chantilly cream (see page 69)

For chocolate or coffee glacé icing
3 squares (3 oz) semisweet chocolate, melted in 1½ tablespoons water, or 1½ tablespoons instant coffee, dissolved in 2 tablespoons water
3 cups confectioners' sugar, sifted
3–4 tablespoons sugar syrup or water

Pastry bag; ½ inch and small plain tubes

Method
Set oven at hot (400°F).
Prepare choux pastry dough and, using a pastry bag fitted with a ½ inch plain tube, pipe the dough fairly far apart onto dampened baking sheets in 3 inch lengths. Bake 10 minutes in the heated oven, then raise the temperature to 425°F and continue baking for about 15 minutes. When éclairs are firm and crisp, prick the sides to release steam and cool on a wire rack. Slit them along one side.
Make the chocolate or coffee pastry cream, if using. Fill the éclairs with pastry cream or Chantilly cream, making sure the whole length is filled, preferably using a pastry bag fitted with a small plain tube.
To make the chocolate glacé icing: in a pan over gentle heat, melt the chocolate in the water, stirring until it is smooth. Take from the heat and beat in the confectioners' sugar. Add enough sugar syrup or water to make a thick cream. Heat the icing over a pan of hot water until warm to the touch – it should coat the back of a spoon. If it is too thick, add a little more syrup or water; if too thin, beat in more confectioners' sugar.
Dip the top of the éclairs in the icing and leave on a wire rack to set.
For coffee éclairs make the coffee glacé icing by omitting chocolate from the method above and instead using the instant coffee dissolved in 2 tablespoons water.

Salambos

4–5 egg quantity of choux pastry (see page 78)
¾ cup sugar (for caramel topping)

For orange cream
1 orange
4–6 cubes of sugar
1 teaspoon rum or brandy (optional)
1½ cups heavy cream, whipped until it holds a soft shape

Pastry bag; ⅜ inch and small plain tubes

This is a variation of the traditional salambos that are filled with pastry cream flavored with kirsch and then topped with icing.

Method
Set oven at hot (400°F).
Prepare the choux pastry dough. Pipe it out into small 1–1½ inch mounds, fairly far apart on dampened baking sheets. Bake 10 minutes in the heated oven, then raise the temperature to 425°F and bake 10–20 minutes longer. When the salambos are crisp, prick the sides to release the steam and cool them on a wire rack.

To make the caramel topping: put the sugar in a small, heavy-based pan and cook slowly until it melts and forms a rich brown syrup.
Watchpoint: immediately stop the caramel cooking by dipping the bottom of the pan in warm water.
Dip the top of each salambo quickly into the caramel while it is still warm and liquid.
To make the orange cream: rub sugar cubes over the orange rind to remove all the zest (the oil in orange rind), then crush the cubes and mix with a little juice from the orange to make a rich syrup. Add rum or brandy if you like. Gradually beat the orange syrup into the whipped cream.
Watchpoint: add this syrup carefully because the whipped cream can curdle if it is beaten too much.
Make slits in the sides of the salambos and fill with the orange cream, preferably using a pastry bag fitted with a small plain tube.

Chocolate Profiteroles

4–5 egg quantity of choux
   pastry (see page 78)
2 cups chocolate pastry cream
   (see page 79)

For Suchard sauce
6 squares (6 oz) unsweetened
   chocolate, chopped
$1\frac{1}{2}$ cups water
$\frac{1}{2}$ cup sugar
pinch of salt
$\frac{1}{2}$ teaspoon vanilla

*Pastry bag; $\frac{3}{8}$ inch and small
   plain tubes (optional)*

Method
Set oven at hot (400°F).
   Prepare the choux pastry dough. Pipe into small 1–1$\frac{1}{2}$ inch mounds, using a $\frac{3}{8}$ inch plain tube, or shape the dough with a teaspoon and set fairly far apart on dampened baking sheets. Bake 10 minutes in the heated oven, then raise the temperature to 425°F and bake 10–20 minutes longer. When profiteroles are crisp and firm to the touch, prick the sides to release steam and cool them on a wire rack.
   Prepare the chocolate pastry cream and reserve.
   To make Suchard sauce: melt chocolate with the water in a pan over low heat, stirring occasionally. When smooth, add the sugar and salt (salt improves sweet things like chocolate sauce) and stir until dissolved. Bring sauce to a boil and simmer, uncovered, until syrupy and of a coating consistency. Take from heat and add vanilla. Leave to cool.
   Make a slit in the side of each profiterole and fill with the chocolate pastry cream, preferably using a pastry bag fitted with a small plain tube. Pile the profiteroles in a pyramid in a serving dish and spoon the sauce over the top.

Choux Pralinés Montmorency

4–5 egg quantity of choux
    pastry (see page 78)
1 tablespoon finely chopped
    blanched almonds
1 teaspoon sugar
1½ cups heavy cream, stiffly
    whipped
confectioners' sugar
    (for sprinkling)

For praline
¼ cup whole unblanched
    almonds
¼ cup sugar

For cherry sauce
1 can (16 oz) pitted cherries
    in light syrup
2 teaspoons arrowroot
½ cup red wine
3 tablespoons red currant jelly
grated rind of 1 orange

*Pastry bag; ⅜ inch and small
    plain tubes (optional)*

Montmorency is the name of
a variety of cherry grown
around Paris.

Method
Set oven at hot (400°F).
    To make the praline: put
the unblanched almonds and
sugar in a small, heavy-based
pan and cook slowly to a rich
brown syrup, stirring occasionally. Pour at once into an
oiled cake pan and, when cool
and hard, grind with a rotary
grater or work, a little at a
time, in a blender.
    Prepare the choux pastry
dough, but reserve about 1
teaspoon of the beaten egg.
Pipe the dough into small
1–1½ inch mounds using a
pastry bag fitted with a ⅜ inch
plain tube, or shape dough
with a teaspoon, placing
mounds fairly far apart on
dampened baking sheets.
Brush tops with reserved egg
and sprinkle with the almonds.

Bake 10 minutes in heated
oven, then raise temperature
to 425°F and continue baking
about 15 minutes. When crisp
and firm to the touch, prick
sides to release steam, and
cool on a wire rack.
    Beat the sugar into the
whipped cream and fold in
praline. Make a small hole in
the choux and fill with the
cream, preferably using a
pastry bag fitted with a small
plain tube. Pile on a platter
and sprinkle generously with
confectioners' sugar.
    To make the cherry sauce:
drain juice from the cherries,
stir a little into the arrowroot
to form a smooth paste and
stir into remaining juice.
Bring the mixture to a boil,
stirring until it thickens, and
cool.
    Boil the wine in a pan until
reduced by half, add the red
currant jelly and melt it slowly.
Add this to the thickened
cherry juice and, when cold,
stir in the cherries and grated
orange rind. Serve the sauce
separately with the choux
puffs.

SAVORY CHOUX

One of the most popular
recipes for savory choux is
called gougère – choux pastry
dough mixed with cheese.
This pastry is served plain as
an hors d'œuvre or with a
savory filling as a supper dish.
Gougère originated in Burgundy, but is now served in
many parts of France.

Shrimp Gougère

For choux pastry
⅔ cup flour
pinch of salt
⅔ cup water
⅓ cup butter
3–4 eggs
½ cup diced Cheddar cheese
pepper

For shrimp filling
1½ cups (½ lb) peeled, cooked
    shrimps
1 medium onion, sliced
1 tablespoon butter
2 teaspoons flour
1½ cups fish or chicken stock
    or milk
2 tomatoes, peeled, seeded
    and cut in strips
2 tablespoons chopped
    parsley
2 tablespoons grated Parmesan
    cheese
2 tablespoons browned
    breadcrumbs

*8–9 inch pie pan or baking dish,
    or 6 individual baking dishes*

Method
Prepare the choux pastry
dough and, after adding the
beaten eggs, stir in the diced
Cheddar cheese and season to
taste.
    Set the oven at moderately
hot (375°F).

    To make the shrimp filling:
cook the onion in the butter
until soft but not browned.
Take the pan from the heat,
stir in the flour and pour in
the stock or milk. Bring to a
boil, stirring, and simmer 2
minutes. Take from the heat,
add the shrimps, tomatoes,
1 tablespoon parsley and
season well.
    Butter the pie pan or
baking dish or individual
dishes generously and arrange
the choux pastry dough
around the sides, hollowing
out the center.
    Pour the filling into the
hollows and sprinkle with
grated Parmesan cheese and
browned breadcrumbs, mixed
together. Bake in heated
oven for 30–40 minutes for
a large gougère or 15–20
minutes for individual ones
or until puffed and brown.
    Sprinkle the gougère with
chopped parsley before serving. Serves 6.

Gougère with Chicken Livers, Game or Ham

For choux pastry
$\frac{2}{3}$ cup flour
$\frac{2}{3}$ cup water
$\frac{1}{3}$ cup butter
$\frac{1}{2}$ cup diced Cheddar cheese
3–4 eggs
salt and pepper

For filling
1 cup chicken livers, or cooked game or ham, cut in strips
$\frac{1}{4}$ cup butter
2 medium onions, sliced or chopped
4–6 mushrooms, sliced
1 tablespoon flour
1 cup stock
2 tomatoes, peeled, seeded and cut in strips
2 tablespoons grated Parmesan cheese
2 tablespoons browned breadcrumbs
2 teaspoons chopped parsley

8–9 inch pie pan or baking dish, or 8 individual soufflé dishes

Method
Prepare choux pastry dough and, after adding the beaten eggs, stir in the cheese. Season to taste.

To make the filling: melt half the butter and, if using chicken livers, sauté them briskly for about 3 minutes until brown on all sides. Remove them, add the remaining butter to pan and cook the onions slowly until soft. Add the mushrooms and cook 2 minutes or until tender. Take the pan from the heat, stir in the flour and pour on the stock. Bring to a boil and simmer 2 minutes, stirring constantly. Take the pan from the heat, add the cooked livers, game or ham and the tomatoes, and season to

taste.

Set oven at hot (400°F).

Thoroughly grease the pie pan, baking dish or soufflé dishes, and arrange the dough around the sides, leaving a hollow in the center. Pour the filling into this and sprinkle with the cheese mixed with the browned breadcrumbs.

Bake in heated oven for 30–40 minutes (15–20 minutes for individual dishes) until the gougère is puffed and brown. Sprinkle with chopped parsley before serving.

Cheese Gougère

$\frac{2}{3}$ cup flour
$\frac{2}{3}$ cup milk
$\frac{1}{3}$ cup butter
$\frac{1}{2}$ cup diced Cheddar cheese
3–4 eggs
salt and pepper
1 egg, beaten to mix

8–9 inch pie pan or oval baking dish

Method
Set the oven at hot (400°F).

Make the pastry dough as for choux pastry, using milk instead of water. Stir in the cheese after the eggs and season well to taste.

Well grease the pan or dish and spread the dough inside, leaving the center slightly hollow. Pour over the beaten egg and bake in the heated oven for 25 minutes until the gougère is puffed and brown. Serve at once with hot tomato sauce.

Marjolaine Tartlets

For choux pastry
$\frac{2}{3}$ cup flour
$\frac{2}{3}$ cup water
$\frac{1}{3}$ cup butter
$\frac{1}{2}$ cup grated Cheddar cheese
3–4 eggs
salt and pepper

1 cup quantity of rich pie pastry (made with $\frac{1}{3}$ cup butter, 1 cup flour sifted with $\frac{1}{4}$ teaspoon salt, 1 egg yolk, 1–2 tablespoons water)

For cheese sauce
6 tablespoons grated Parmesan cheese
1 tablespoon butter
1 tablespoon flour
$1\frac{1}{4}$ cups milk (infused with 1 bay leaf, slice of onion, blade of mace, 6 peppercorns)

6–8 tartlet pans; pastry bag and $\frac{1}{4}$ inch plain tube

Method
Set the oven at moderately hot (375°F).

To make rich pie pastry: cut the butter into the flour until in small pieces and well coated. Then rub in with the fingertips until the mixture looks like crumbs. Make a well in the center and add egg yolk and water and stir to combine. Draw the flour into the mixture in the center quickly with a knife, adding more water if necessary to form a smooth dough.

Turn onto a floured board or marble slab and knead pie pastry dough lightly until smooth. Wrap in wax paper, plastic wrap or a plastic bag. Chill 30 minutes before using.

Line the tartlets pans with the rich pie pastry dough. Prick the bottoms, line with foil or silicone paper, fill with rice or beans and bake blind

in heated oven for 10–15 minutes or until golden. Cool.

Prepare the choux pastry dough and, after adding the beaten eggs, beat in the cheese with seasoning to taste. Pipe the dough, using the pastry bag fitted with a $\frac{1}{4}$ inch plain tube, into the baked tartlet shells, leaving a hollow in the center of each one. Turn up the oven to hot (400°F).

To make the cheese sauce: melt the butter in a saucepan, stir in the flour and cook the roux until it is straw-colored. Strain the infused milk and stir it into the roux. Bring to a boil, stirring, and simmer for 2 minutes. Stir in the cheese, off the heat, and season to taste.

Pour the cheese sauce into the hollows in the tartlets and bake in heated oven for 15–20 minutes until the choux dough is puffed and brown and the sauce in the middle of the tartlets is brown. Serve immediately.

Choux pastry

Gougère, with chicken liver, mushrooms, tomatoes and onions, is topped with breadcrumbs and cheese

Cheese beignets are delicious as a hot appetizer

Cheese Profiteroles

3–4 egg quantity of choux
   pastry (see page 78)
½ cup freshly grated
   Parmesan cheese
pinch of cayenne
pinch of dry mustard
salt and pepper
little beaten egg (for glaze)

To serve
1–2 tablespoons grated
   Parmesan cheese
1 tablespoon chopped parsley

Method
Set oven at hot (400°F).

Make choux pastry dough, reserving a little of the last egg for the glaze, add cheese, reserving 2 tablespoons, with cayenne and mustard and season highly. Put heaping teaspoonsful of the dough well apart on dampened baking sheets, brush lightly with beaten egg and sprinkle with reserved cheese. Bake 10 minutes in heated oven, then raise temperature to 425°F and continue baking 10–20 minutes.

When the profiteroles are crisp and firm to the touch, remove them, prick the sides to release steam and serve hot. Sprinkle with more grated Parmesan cheese and chopped parsley. Serve with tomato sauce, if you like.

Fried Choux

Deep-fried choux pastry puffs, called beignets soufflés or fritters, may be served with a jam or fruit sauce as a hot dessert or they may be flavored with cheese for a savory dish. Small cheese beignets make excellent cocktail hors d'œuvre. Like all deep-fried foods, beignets must be thoroughly drained and are at their best served immediately.

Beignets Soufflés

3–4 egg quantity of choux
   pastry (see page 78)
granulated sugar
   (for sprinkling)
hot jam sauce (for serving)

Method
Prepare choux pastry dough. Divide the dough into heaping teaspoons on a dish or pan.

Heat the deep fat to 350°F on a fat thermometer. Dip a metal spatula into the fat and use this to lift each spoonful of dough from the dish or pan into the fat. Do not fry too many beignets at a time as they swell. They will turn over automatically as they puff if there is plenty of room in the pan.

Once the dough is added, increase the heat gradually to 375°F and continue cooking about 5–6 minutes until the pastry is golden brown and firm to the touch.

Lift out the beignets with a slotted spoon and drain them on paper towels. Sprinkle generously with sugar and serve at once with hot jam sauce.

Hot Jam Sauce

½ cup jam (apricot,
   raspberry or pineapple)
¼ cup water
juice of 1 lemon

Method
Put the jam, water and lemon juice in a pan and heat gently until the jam is dissolved. Bring to a boil, take from the heat and strain. Return the sauce to the pan, bring just to a boil and serve.

Cheese Beignets

Make 3–4 egg quantity of choux pastry dough (see page 78) but mix in 2 tablespoons finely grated Parmesan or dry Cheddar cheese before frying. Fry as for beignets soufflés. After draining, sprinkle them with grated Parmesan cheese and cayenne before serving.

Sprinkle cheese beignets with grated Parmesan cheese and cayenne before serving

HOW TO USE A FREEZER

Freezing is probably the safest method of preserving food at home and it is certainly one of the easiest. With very little preparation you can store large quantities of food for months at a time without danger of deterioration. You can take advantage of special offers on meat and poultry and buy large quantities of seasonal fresh vegetables and fruit when they are least expensive and at their best.

When food is frozen, the low temperatures hold back the active life of plant and animal tissue. Fast freezing and low storage temperatures check the growth of micro-organisms (yeasts, molds and bacteria) that cause changes in the color, flavor and texture of food. Ideally, home freezers should operate at −12°F or lower while food is being frozen; then store it at 0°F. Commercial freezers operate at even lower temperatures, around −20°F.

Once food is thawed, it spoils rapidly, so use it at once; never refreeze anything except raw food that can be thawed, cooked, and then refrozen.

Remember, you cannot improve the quality of food by freezing it, so use only fresh, top quality foods and prepare, package and freeze them as soon as possible. For individual items, follow the charts on pages 92–94; apart from fruits and vegetables, few foods need special treatment. For advice on freezer wraps and containers, see page 94. Recipes that are good for freezing will be given in a future Volume.

Points to remember

1 Color, flavor, texture and nutritive value of food are affected if it is stored at temperatures above 0°F, or if it is put to freeze at above –5°F.

2 Freeze food quickly to prevent large ice crystals from forming. (The finer the ice crystals, the less chance of damage to cells in tissues of food.)

3 Do not freeze too much at once to allow the temperature of the freezer to stay low and so food is frozen as quickly as possible. Two pounds of food per cubic foot of freezer space is enough to add at a time. When frozen, food can be packed tightly in the freezer.

4 Food should be thawed slowly, preferably in the refrigerator. Allow 12 hours for small packages and 24–36 hours for large roasts and casseroles. Vegetables (other than corn on the cob) are an exception – cook them straight from the freezer.

5 As a general rule, the larger the item, the longer it can be kept; beef roasts can be stored up to a year, but steaks should be used within 6 months and ground beef within 2 months.

6 Thickened liquids tend to thicken on freezing, so prepare sauces slightly thinner than usual. Sauces with egg yolks and cream must be reheated in a double boiler and stirred often to prevent separation.

7 Seasonings taste stronger after freezing; use salt, pepper, garlic and spices sparingly. Others lose flavor, such as cinnamon, chili, onion and soy sauce.

8 Label packages clearly so they can be thawed in rotation. It helps to keep a list and cross off items when used.

9 Freezing does not preserve food indefinitely despite low temperatures, so keep to the storage periods recommended in the charts on pages 92–94.

10 Some frozen foods that are available in markets should not be frozen at home – clams in the shell and turkeys with stuffing are examples. These are 'flash frozen' commercially at much lower temperatures than a home freezer can reach.

11 Pack and wrap food carefully. Packages must be airtight and vapor-moisture-proof to prevent the oxidation and evaporation that cause white patches called 'freezer burns'. Vapor-moistureproof wrappings also prevent transfer of flavors from one package to another. Exclude as much air from a package as possible unless contents are liquid and likely to expand on freezing – if this is the case leave a space at the top of container for expansion. If packing sharp items like meat with bones, use a durable wrap that does not tear easily.

IF ELECTRICITY IS CUT OFF: leave the door of the freezer closed; food should keep 1–2 days without harm; the exact time depends on room temperature and quantity of food – the more there is, the longer it will keep. After that, examine packages – if they are still hard in the center, showing they contain ice crystals, it is safe to refreeze them although flavor may be affected. Food which is completely defrosted must be used at once.

DO NOT FREEZE THESE FOODS:

1 Egg-based Hollandaise sauces like mayonnaise or egg custard.
2 Crisp raw salad vegetables like lettuce, celery, radishes, cucumbers, cabbage, onions, green peppers and tomatoes. (Tomatoes can be frozen as a purée or sauce, or quartered for cooking.)
3 Whole bananas (mashed ones can be frozen).
4 Buttermilk, sour cream, yogurt.
5 Shellfish like oysters and clams in the shell.
6 Eggs in shells.
7 Glacé and fondant icings.
8 Mixtures containing vinegar in foil containers as the metal may affect flavor.

Meat and Game

Chill meat thoroughly, divide into suitable cuts and trim excess bones and fat. Separate chops or small pieces of meat with sheets of wax paper or plastic wrap so the package can be divided when frozen. Wrap in vapor-moistureproof wrap, squeezing the package well to remove as much air as possible. Fasten with freezer tape and label.

Ground meats dehydrate more easily than larger cuts so wrap them well.

Variety Meats

Chill, then package them in plastic or wax containers.

Separate slices of liver with wax paper and wrap in freezer wrap.

Ham, Bacon and Smoked Meats

Ham, bacon, sausages and other meats cured with salt oxidize more quickly when frozen than uncured meat. Freeze them for a maximum of 2 months and only when really necessary.

Poultry and Game Birds

Truss whole birds (never stuff them before freezing) and wrap in heavy duty foil or vapor-moistureproof wrap or in freezer bags. Press to exclude air. Freeze giblets separately.

If space is limited, cut up large birds and freeze only the best portions.

Use the backbones, wings and necks to make stock, reduce it well and freeze.

Eggs

Whole eggs freeze well but they crack if left in the shell. To prevent the eggs from coagulating add $\frac{1}{2}$ teaspoon salt or 2 teaspoons sugar to every cup of whole eggs (about 5) or to every $\frac{1}{2}$ cup egg yolks (7–8 yolks) and beat lightly to mix. Egg whites can be frozen plain.

When freezing a liquid like eggs, leave room for expansion at the top of the container.

Hard-cooked eggs do not freeze well.

Dairy Products

Unsalted butter freezes better than butter with salt – be sure it is well wrapped and cannot absorb flavors from other packages.

Do not freeze cream unless it contains more than 40% butterfat as it separates when thawed. Whipped cream tends to separate when frozen in large quantities, but small rosettes of cream can be frozen successfully: pipe rosettes onto a baking sheet and freeze until hard. Lift them from the baking sheet, pack in a container or freezer bag and use as needed – the rosettes will thaw within 10 minutes and should not be left to stand for too long.

Cheeses can be frozen but they tend to lose flavor and change texture.

Homogenized milk can be frozen but its flavor will be altered and it should be used only for cooking.

Buttermilk, sour cream and yogurt cannot be frozen.

Fish and Shellfish

If the fish is freshly caught, clean and prepare it for cooking. Leave whole or skin it and cut in fillets, as you like. Chill thoroughly and wrap large whole fish individually in vapor-moistureproof wrap; pack small fish and fillets in plastic or wax containers, with sheets of wax paper between the layers. Rich fish like salmon cannot be kept as long as white fish.

Shrimps should be frozen in the shell, whether cooked or uncooked, as this protects them from dehydration. Pack them in containers or freezer bags, excluding as much air as possible.

Freshly cooked lobsters and crabs may be frozen in the shell or the meat may be removed from the shell.

Oysters and clams should be as fresh as possible. They must be shucked, then packed in containers or freezer bags.

Herbs

Herbs can be frozen, but do not blanch them. Crumbling parsley while still frozen will have the effect of chopping it.

Vegetables

Some enzymes keep working at very low temperatures, so most vegetables must be blanched before freezing to stop this action. Blanch the vegetables quickly, otherwise nutrients are lost. Do this in small quantities so that once added to boiling water they reboil as soon as possible.

Use a large kettle and allow 2 gallons (8 quarts) water per lb of vegetables. For easy handling, place the vegetables in a wire basket. Put them in boiling water; count the blanching time (see chart on page 92) from the moment the water comes back to a boil. When completed, cool the vegetables quickly by plunging them in ice water. When blanched quickly like this, vegetables lose the minimum of vitamins. The same water can be used for blanching 6–7 times.

Pack the vegetables in freezer bags, plastic or wax containers, fasten with freezer tape and label.

Fruits

Soft fruits like strawberries are best frozen dry without sugar or syrup. Wash and dry fruits thoroughly; place, without fruits touching, on a baking sheet or pan and freeze for 2–3 hours or until very hard. Pack in vapor-moisture-proof containers or in freezer bags, excluding as much air as possible, seal and label.

Most other fruits must be frozen with dry sugar, which draws the juice from the fruit to form a syrup, or with a sugar syrup. Sugar syrup protects the surface of fruit from oxidizing and turning brown and retards, to some extent, enzyme action during storage.

Some light-colored fruit, e.g. peaches, turn brown quickly once cut, so add a small amount of ascorbic acid (available at pharmacies). For syrup pack, add $\frac{1}{2}$ teaspoon ascorbic acid crystals per quart of fruit to the syrup before it is added to the fruit. If using dry sugar, dissolve $\frac{1}{4}$ teaspoon ascorbic acid per quart of fruit in 2 tablespoons cold water and sprinkle over the fruit before adding the sugar. Pack in freezer bags or plastic or wax containers, fasten with freezer tape and label.

Do not attempt to freeze any damaged or over- or underripe fruit.

COOKED FOODS

All baked goods freeze well. Breads and rolls should be wrapped in freezer bags and frozen as soon as possible after baking. Yeast rolls and small yeast coffeecakes can be half-baked and then frozen; bake them in a low oven (300°F) for 20 minutes, then cool and freeze. To complete the baking, thaw them for 10 minutes, then bake in a very hot oven (450°F) for 5–10 minutes or until brown.

All kinds of cakes (even filled with a cooked or butter frosting), muffins and cup-cakes freeze well, but glacé and fondant icings will crack, and whipped cream fillings will separate.

Pies can be frozen, baked or unbaked, in foil pans – although baked pies are generally considered to freeze best. To store a large quantity of filling – without the pans: line the pie pan with foil, leaving at least 6 inches over-lap at the rim. Add the filling

continued on next page

and fold the extra foil on top. Freeze until the filling is firm, then remove the foil-wrapped filling from the pan and wrap in a freezer bag. To bake the pie, line pie pan with pastry, put the unwrapped filling on top and let thaw. Cover with pastry if you like, and bake.

Sandwiches freeze well providing they are not filled with a moist mixture that will make the bread soggy, nor with hard-cooked eggs that toughen when frozen. For packed lunches and picnics the freezer is invaluable; sandwiches taken from the freezer in the morning will be thawed by lunchtime.

Freeze sandwich fillings in containers in the quantity

FREEZING CHART FOR VEGETABLES (all vegetables should be washed)

TYPE OF FOOD	STORAGE TIME	PREPARATION	BLANCHING/COOKING TIME
Asparagus	9–12 months	trim	2–4 minutes
Beans, green	1 year	top and tail, slice or leave whole	1–2 minutes, sliced; 3 minutes, whole
Beans, lima	1 year	shell	2–3 minutes
Beets (small)	6 months	cook, peel, slice or dice	—
Broccoli	1 year	cut into 4 inch sprigs	3 minutes
Brussels sprouts	1 year	pick over and trim	3–5 minutes
Cabbage	6–8 months	shred	$1\frac{1}{2}$ minutes; use only as a cooked vegetable
Carrots (small)	6 months	scrape; slice or dice if large	2–3 minutes
Cauliflower	6 months	cut into flowerets	3 minutes
Corn (ears)	1 year	shuck and trim	7–11 minutes if left on the cob
Corn (kernels)	6 months	stem; cook, then leave on cob or cut off	4 minutes for kernels
Celery	6 months	dice or slice	3 minutes; use only as a cooked vegetable
Mushrooms	1 year	wash in water with lemon juice, trim stems	steam 3–5 minutes or fry in butter
Peas, green	1 year	shell	$1\frac{1}{2}$ minutes
Peppers	1 year	discard core and seeds, chop or finely slice	1–2 minutes; use only as a cooked vegetable
Pumpkin (purée)	6 months	peel and cut in 1 inch cubes, cook and purée	8 minutes or until tender
Spinach and other greens	1 year	wash and dry	1–3 minutes
Squash, summer	9 months	wash and slice	3 minutes
Squash, winter (purée)	6 months	peel, cut in cubes, cook and purée	8–10 minutes or until tender
Tomatoes (purée)	1 year	scald, peel, remove seeds, cook, purée and sieve	5 minutes
Tomatoes (quartered)	1 year	scald, peel and cook	10–20 minutes; use only as a cooked vegetable

needed. Take them from the freezer and put in refrigerator overnight so filling is ready for spreading in the morning.

Use the freezer for leftovers of all kinds; freeze bread slices and make them into breadcrumbs in a blender while they are still frozen. Freeze small amounts of cooked ham, chicken and other meats, preferably in a sauce, for fillings for crêpes or bouchée cases. Keep leftover mushrooms, etc. for adding to stews. Layer crêpes with wax paper, take them out as needed and thaw them slowly before using.

If a recipe calls for half a green pepper or onion, chop the remainder, blanch it and freeze until needed.

Continued on next page

FREEZING CHART FOR FRUIT (all fruits can be stored for 9–12 months)

TYPE OF FOOD	PREPARATION	PACKING
Apples	pare, core, slice and add ascorbic acid	pack dry with sugar for pies, or cook in light syrup 3 minutes or cook until tender and purée
Apricots	scald, peel, halve and pit and add ascorbic acid	pack dry with sugar, or cover with light or medium syrup
Avocados	peel, remove seed, and purée	add one-eighth teaspoon ascorbic acid or 1 cup sugar per quart of purée
Blackberries	pick over, wash in ice water; dry if necessary	freeze dry with or without sugar, or cover with light syrup
Blueberries	pick over, wash in ice water; dry if necessary	freeze dry with or without sugar, or cover with light syrup
Cherries	remove stems and wash; remove pits (optional) and add ascorbic acid	freeze dry with sugar, or cover with medium syrup
Cranberries	wash and dry	freeze dry without sugar
Figs	wash, halve, slice, or leave whole and add ascorbic acid	cover with light or medium syrup
Grapefruit and oranges	chill, peel, removing pith and cut in sections; add ascorbic acid	cover with light syrup
Grapes	wash and peel; remove seeds, if you like	cover with light syrup
Melon	cut in slices, cubes or balls	cover with light syrup
Nectarines and peaches	scald, peel, halve and pit; slice (optional) and add ascorbic acid	cover with light or medium syrup
Pears	pare, core, slice and add ascorbic acid	cook in light syrup 2 minutes, or cook until tender and purée
Pineapple	remove skin and core, cut in slices or pieces	freeze dry without sugar, or cover with light or medium syrup
Plums	wash, halve and pit; add ascorbic acid	cover with light or medium syrup
Raspberries	pick over; wash only if necessary and dry	freeze dry with or without sugar
Rhubarb	wash and slice	freeze dry with or without sugar, or cover with light syrup
Strawberries	hull; wash in cold water only if necessary, and dry; leave whole or slice	freeze dry with or without sugar, or cover with light or medium syrup

For **light syrup**, allow $\frac{3}{4}$ cup sugar to 2 cups water; for **medium syrup**, $2\frac{1}{2}$ cups sugar to 2 cups water.

When packing dry with sugar, allow about 1 cup sugar for every quart fruit, depending on acidity.

OTHER TYPES OF FOOD AND THEIR STORAGE TIMES

MEAT AND GAME	STORAGE TIME
Beef, game and lamb (roasts and large pieces)	1 year
Pork (roasts and large pieces)	8 months
Variety meats and ground meats	2 months
Stews and casseroles	2 months

POULTRY/GAME BIRDS	STORAGE TIME
Chicken, turkey and other white-fleshed birds	1 year
Duck, geese	6 months
Game birds	6 months
Poultry parts and giblets	3 months

DAIRY PRODUCTS	STORAGE TIME
Butter (unsalted)	6 months
Butter (salted)	3 months
Cheese (hard)	3 months
Cheese (cream and cottage)	1 month
Cream (over 40% butterfat)	2 months
Eggs (without shell)	1 year
Homogenized milk	1 month
Ice cream	1 month

FISH	STORAGE TIME
White	6–9 months
Rich	3 months

SHELLFISH	STORAGE TIME
Shrimps (fresh, unpeeled)	4 months
Shrimps (cooked, unpeeled)	3–4 months
Crabs, lobster (unshelled)	3–4 months
Crabs, lobster (shelled)	1–2 months
Scallops (fresh)	2–3 months
Scallops (cooked)	1–2 months
Oysters, clams (shucked)	1–2 months

MISCELLANEOUS	STORAGE TIME
Bread	3 months
Cakes (frosted or filled)	2 months
Cakes (unfrosted and unfilled)	3 months
Pastry (baked pie shells, etc.)	6 months
Pastry dough (unbaked)	3 months
Sandwiches	3 months
Sauces, soups, stocks	4 months

Cooked foods continued

Do not refreeze leftovers once they have been thawed. Many savory cooked dishes freeze well such as soups and casseroles, particularly if they have a sauce. However, dry cooked meats tend to become tough. Sauces, soups and stocks can be frozen in small containers or in ice cube trays. When hard, transfer for storage to freezer bags. This makes small quantities of sauce and stock readily available. Always skim off as much fat as possible before freezing.

More detailed advice on freezing cooked dishes will be given in a future Volume.

FREEZER WRAPS & CONTAINERS

The freezer wraps and containers you use are the key to successful freezing. Proper wraps keep the foods from drying out and preserve their flavor, color and texture. All materials should be waterproof (to prevent leakage), easy to work with and seal, and durable enough so that they don't become brittle and crack at low temperatures.

It is false economy to use ineffective wrappings such as ordinary wax paper, bread wrappers, paper bags, and regular plastic wraps or containers like ice cream cartons. Instead, buy packaging material (and there are many varieties on the market) that can be used again and again.

Non-rigid or sheet wrappings include vapor-moisture-proof plastic films, freezer aluminum foil, laminated papers, Pliofilm, polyethylene, duplex bags of various combinations of paper, metal, foil, glassine, cellophane and rubber latex . . . all particularly suitable for dry-packed fruits and vegetables.

Rigid containers include aluminum cans, plastic freezer containers, freezer jars, outer waxed cartons (with new liners every time), tin or special enamel-lined cans and glass canning jars that work well when freezing fruits and vegetables (with the exception of those packed in water because water expands as it freezes and may crack the jar).

Packaging for a Freezer

Select the size container that will hold enough food for one meal for your family.

Consider the shape of the container: rigid straight-sided containers that are flat on the top and bottom stack conveniently. Those with flared sides or raised bottoms or that are round in shape all waste freezer space. Other containers that can be used many times are tin cans with slip-top closers, glass and aluminum containers, also folding cardboard cartons used to protect an inner bag.

It is just as important to seal the wrapper or container properly as it is to use the right container. Tops for rigid containers are sealed by pressing or screwing on the lids. Glass jars must be sealed with a rubber ring underneath the lid.

Most freezer bags can be sealed by twisting the tops and folding back the excess before securing it with string, a rubber or plastic band or freezer tape. Some bags have a metal strip attached to the top of the bag for quick closing.

To save space, some foods can be frozen until solid, then removed from their containers and placed in freezer bags. For example, line a casserole with freezer foil, fill it with the mixture, freeze and, when solid, wrap in a bag and store. When ready to use, the mixture will fit neatly into the casserole. Stock can be frozen in ice cube trays for convenience if you need only a little at a time.

Types of Wraps and Containers

The following are wraps or containers for home freezing, with suggestions on what to store in them.

Laminated polyethylene paper, available in rolls, should be used for meat, fish, poultry, baked goods and corn on the cob. Place polyethylene side towards food and seal with freezer tape after wrapping. To label, write directly on the paper, which may be reused if not worn. After use, wipe with a damp cloth and fold.

Plastic bags, available in all sizes, can be used for vegetables, soft fruits packed without sugar or syrup, cookies and small baked goods. After food is in bag, press out air, fold over top and seal with a rubber band or twister. After use, rinse with warm water, dry and store.

Plastic cartons that stack easily when not in use can be used for vegetables, fruits, made-up dishes, casseroles and cookies. Be sure to allow for expansion when freezing liquid and semi-liquid mixtures.

Tin cans, like the type ground coffee comes in, can be used for cookies and shelled meats. Separate layers of cookies or nutmeats with wax paper. Seal lid with freezer tape.

Aluminum foil, available in rolls, comes in light or heavy weight. Aluminum is a good conductor of heat and cold so foods will freeze and defrost quickly. Light weight aluminum can be used for foods stored for a short period of time, otherwise use the heavy weight. Store meat, fish, poultry, baked goods, asparagus, and corn on the cob in aluminum foil. Pad the bones in meat with wax paper to avoid tearing foil. No special sealing is necessary.

Heatproof glass jars, usually used for preserving, can store fruits, vegetables, made-up dishes, soups and sauces. Allow headspace for expansion and handle carefully.

Pliofilm is heavier and sturdier than cellophane and is excellent for wrapping foods with irregular shapes. It needs to be covered and must be heat-sealed.

All packages of food that go into the freezer should be labeled. There are gummed labels, colored tape, freezer tape, crayons, pens and stamps that can be used. On the label include the name of the food, the date it was packed and the method of preparation if the food was packed in more than one form.

Fish en coquille, coated with mayonnaise, is decorated with strips of anchovy fillet (recipe is on page 98)

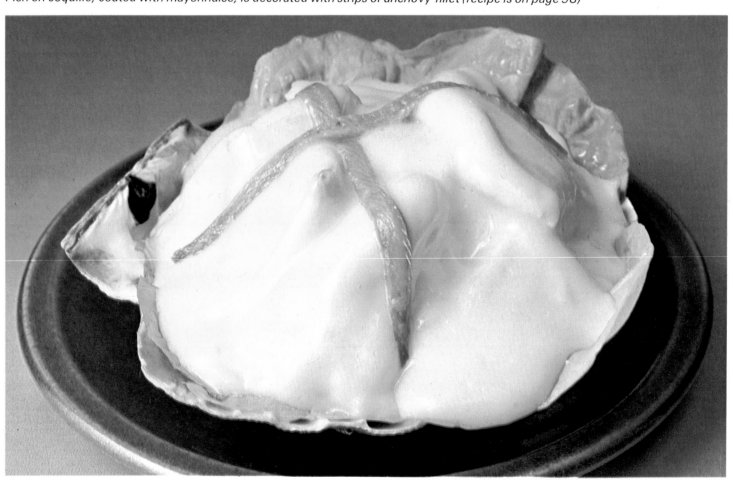

Supper for 24 or even 50 people will be no problem if each cook prepares one or two dishes. Each of the following menus are intended for eight. Select one of four entrées offering a choice of fish in mayonnaise, haddock quiche and two tempting casseroles, with salad accompaniments and desserts for each menu. Just decide which dishes to serve and let three or four cooks prepare the party.

Suppers featuring a host of unrelated entrées provide a problem for the wine connoisseur, but our 18th century forebears suggested a solution with the universal drink — punch! If you have a favorite, make it — as long as it's not too sweet. (A sugary punch would be incompatible with the fish and meat dishes suggested.) If you are without a recipe, try the punch given on page 99.

Alternative Menus

Fish en Coquille
Beet & Green Pea Salad   Cole Slaw
Carrot & Raisin Salad
French Bread
Pineapple Cheesecake

Sausage & Tomato Casserole
Salads (as above)
Sour Cream Mold
with Cranberry and Apple Compote
Quick Nut Bread

Rassolnik Soup
Spaghetti & Ham au Gratin
Salads (as above)
Coffee Gelatin

Smoked Haddock Quiche
German Potato Salad
Hot Herb Loaf
Salads (as above)
Lemon Sponge Pudding
or
Banana Cake

Punch

Bring-a-dish Suppers

MENU 1

> *Fish en Coquille*
>
> *French Bread*
>
> *Cole Slaw*
> *Beet & Green Pea Salad*
> *Carrot & Raisin Salad*
>
> *Pineapple Cheesecake*

TIMETABLE

Fish en Coquille
Cook the fish and flake it in the morning. Make the mayonnaise, prepare the cucumbers and wash lettuce in the morning. Cover and refrigerate all ingredients. Complete the dish as late as possible.

Salads
Prepare the cooked vegetables, mayonnaise and dressings the day before. Cover and refrigerate overnight.
Prepare the raw vegetables and complete salads in the afternoon. Add garnishes like parsley before serving.

Pineapple Cheesecake
Make and bake the cheesecake in the morning. Add pineapple topping and glaze 1–2 hours before serving.

Entrée

Fish en Coquille

3 lb white fish fillets
salt
juice of 1 lemon
2 cucumbers, peeled and diced
black pepper, freshly ground
2 teaspoons chopped parsley
2 teaspoons mixed chopped
   mint and chives
1 teaspoon white wine vinegar
2–3 tablespoons boiling water
2 cups mayonnaise
   (see page 38)
8 lettuce leaves
16 anchovy fillets, soaked in a
   little milk to remove excess
   salt

8 deep scallop shells or
* individual dishes*

Method
Set oven at moderate (350°F).
  Wipe the fish with paper towels and put in a well-buttered baking dish. Sprinkle with a little salt and lemon juice and cover with buttered paper or foil. Bake in heated oven for 15–20 minutes, depending on the thickness of the fish, or until it flakes easily when tested with a fork. Leave to cool.
  Sprinkle the cucumbers with salt and let stand in a cool place for about 30 minutes. Rinse with cold water, drain thoroughly and season with pepper, herbs and wine vinegar. Stir enough boiling water into the mayonnaise to give it a coating consistency.
  Place a lettuce leaf in each scallop shell or dish and add a spoonful of seasoned cucumber. When the fish is cold, remove any skin and bones and carefully flake the flesh with a fork. Arrange the fish in individual shells or dishes and coat with mayonnaise. Drain anchovy fillets and arrange them on top of each shell in an X pattern. The fish may also be arranged in a large dish, if you like.

Flake the cooled fish before arranging it in scallop shells on lettuce leaves and with the chopped cucumber

Coat the fish with mayonnaise and place the anchovy fillets in an X pattern on top

Accompaniments to entrée

Beet and Green Pea Salad

1½ cups diced, cooked beets
1½ cups cooked peas
1½ cups diced, cooked potatoes
4 hard-cooked eggs, chopped
1 cup mayonnaise (see
   page 38)
3 scallions, chopped

Method
Mix the beets, peas, potatoes and chopped hard-cooked eggs together with the mayonnaise. Put salad into a bowl and sprinkle with scallions.

Cole Slaw

1 medium head of firm green
   cabbage
1 cup boiled dressing or ¾ cup
   vinaigrette dressing (see
   page 38)
salt and pepper
1 dessert apple
3 medium carrots, grated
   (optional)
½ teaspoon paprika, or 1
   tablespoon chopped parsley

Method
Cut the cabbage into four, trim away the hard core and slice cabbage into shreds. Put into a bowl, add the boiled or vinaigrette dressing and extra seasoning to taste. Toss the salad until the cabbage is well coated with dressing.
  Core and thinly slice the apple but do not pare it, and add to the salad with the grated carrots (if used). Mix well, cover and let stand 2–3 hours before serving. Pile in a salad bowl and sprinkle with paprika or parsley.

Carrot and Raisin Salad

10–12 medium carrots
1½ cups raisins
juice of 3 oranges
¾ cup vinaigrette dressing (see page 38)

Method

Wash the raisins in hot water, drain, cover with orange juice and let soak for 1 hour or until they are plump. Peel the carrots and grate coarsely. Mix them with the raisins and enough vinaigrette dressing to moisten the salad.

Dessert

Pineapple Cheesecake

For pastry
1 cup flour
pinch of salt
1 teaspoon sugar
¼ cup butter
1 tablespoon shortening
1 tablespoon white vinegar
1 tablespoon milk

For filling
1 medium fresh pineapple or 1 can (8 oz) pineapple
2 packages (8 oz and 3 oz) cream cheese
3 tablespoons sugar
3 egg yolks
½ cup heavy cream
1 teaspoon vanilla
sugar (for sprinkling)
¾ cup pineapple jam (for glaze)

9 inch springform pan

Method

To make the pastry dough: sift the flour with the salt and sugar, rub in the butter and shortening with the fingertips, then mix in the vinegar and milk to make a firm dough. Roll out pastry onto the base of the springform pan and prick the base lightly with a fork.

Set oven at moderately hot (375°F).

To make the filling: in a bowl beat the cream cheese until smooth, add the sugar, egg yolks, cream and vanilla and stir until well mixed.

Pour the mixture into the springform pan and bake in heated oven for 25–35 minutes or until the mixture is firm to the touch and begins to shrink from the sides of the pan. Cool before removing the pan.

Cut the skin from the pineapple, slice flesh and remove core; sprinkle the slices with sugar. Or drain the canned pineapple.

When cheesecake is cool, overlap slices of pineapple on top. Melt the pineapple jam and work it through a strainer. Reheat this and brush it over the pineapple and cheesecake.

If you wish to double this recipe bake as 2 cakes.

The menus on pages 98–105 serve 8 people.

Many recipes can be doubled or tripled without difficulty. However, to avoid the problems involved in large-scale cooking, we suggest you ask other people to cook 1–2 dishes each and, with very little effort, you can provide enough food for 24 people or even more.

Mix the sugar, egg yolks, cream and vanilla into the beaten cream cheese to make the filling for pineapple cheesecake

After brushing with pineapple jam glaze, the cheesecake is ready for serving

Arrange sugared pineapple slices overlapping on top of the cooled cheesecake

Punch for Bring-a-dish Suppers

Make 1 quart strong tea using ¼ cup loose tea or 8 tea bags. Cool and add the juice of 3 lemons and a 6 oz can of frozen orange-pineapple concentrate.

For a non-alcoholic brew, stir in 3 quarts apple cider and sugar to taste.

If you prefer something more potent, add instead 1 pint brandy and ½ gallon dry white wine with ⅓ cup of sugar; chill.

Just before serving, dilute with 2 quarts of soda water and pour the punch on the rocks in tall glasses.

MENU 2

Salads (prepare as for Menu 1)

Sausage & Tomato
Casserole

Cole Slaw
Beet & Green Pea Salad
Carrot & Raisin Salad

Sour Cream Mold
with Cranberry & Apple
Compote
Quick Nut Bread

TIMETABLE

Sausage and Tomato Casserole
Prepare the mixture in the morning, put in the casserole but do not add the topping until baking time. Bake 30–40 minutes before serving; if transporting the casserole to another house, wrap it in layers of newspaper to keep hot. Or, as suggested in the recipe, omit topping and reheat mixture in a saucepan.

Salads (prepare as for Menu 1)

Quick Nut Bread
Bake day before and keep in airtight container.

Sour Cream Mold
Prepare in the morning. Unmold about 1 hour before serving; cover with whipped cream, if you like.

Cranberry and Apple Compote
Prepare in the morning and refrigerate.

Entrée

Sausage and Tomato Casserole

2 lb pork sausages
6 cups (3 lb) canned tomatoes
3 tablespoons oil
3 large onions, chopped
3 tablespoons flour
3 green peppers, cored, seeded and chopped
salt and pepper
$1\frac{1}{2}$ tablespoons Worcestershire sauce
1 bay leaf
sugar (to taste)
$\frac{1}{4}$ cup browned breadcrumbs (optional)
2 tablespoons grated Parmesan cheese (optional)

Method
Heat the oil in a pan, add the onions and cook over a low heat until golden. Stir in the flour, add the tomatoes and peppers and stir until the mixture comes to a boil. Season, add Worcestershire sauce, bay leaf and sugar to taste. Simmer the mixture for 30–40 minutes.

Parboil the sausages for 10 minutes and when cool enough to handle, remove the skins. Cut the sausages into thick, diagonal slices. Set oven at moderately hot (375°F).

Remove the bay leaf from the sauce. Add the sausages and transfer the mixture to a shallow casserole. Sprinkle the top with breadcrumbs and cheese and bake in heated oven 30 minutes. Or, omit the topping and reheat the mixture in a saucepan before serving.

If doubling the recipe, bake in 2 casseroles.

Dessert

Sour Cream Mold

2 cups sour cream
1 envelope gelatin
$\frac{1}{4}$ cup water
2 cups heavy cream
1 cup sugar
2 tablespoons kirsch or brandy
1 cup heavy cream, whipped until it holds a soft shape (to serve) – optional

*Shallow soufflé dish or mold
($1\frac{1}{2}$ quart capacity)*

Method
Lightly oil the soufflé dish or mold.

In a pan sprinkle the gelatin over the water and stand 5 minutes or until spongy.

Combine the heavy cream and sugar in a saucepan and heat until the sugar dissolves; stir in the softened gelatin. Take from the heat and add the sour cream and liqueur.

Pour into the prepared soufflé dish or mold and chill until firm. Unmold, coat with whipped cream, if you like, and serve with cranberry and apple compote.

If doubling the recipe, set it in 2 molds.

This menu serves eight people. Many of the recipes can be doubled or tripled without difficulty. For **salad recipes** see pages 98–99.

Cranberry and Apple Compote

1 lb cranberries
4 Golden Delicious apples
1 cup sugar
1 cup water

Method
Dissolve the sugar in the water over low heat, then boil 2–3 minutes to make a light syrup. Pare, quarter and core the apples and slice each quarter in half. Add to the syrup, cover and poach gently for 10–12 minutes or until just tender. Draw the pan aside and cool, uncovered.

Carefully lift out the apples, put them into a serving bowl, add the cranberries to the syrup and simmer 5 minutes. Pour over the apples and chill before serving with sour cream mold or ladyfingers and whipped cream.

Sour cream mold is served with cranberry and apple compote

Quick Nut Bread

½ cup whole, blanched almonds
½ cup chopped pecans
1 cup flour
2 teaspoons baking powder
1 teaspoon salt
½ cup wholewheat flour
1 tablespoon sugar
3 eggs
¼ cup melted shortening
1 cup milk

Medium loaf pan (8½ X 2½ X 4½ inches)

Method

Set oven at moderately low (325°F) and grease the loaf pan.

Finely grind the almonds and pecans.

Sift the flour with the baking powder and salt; stir in the wholewheat flour and sugar. Make a well in the center, add the eggs, melted shortening and milk. Gradually stir in the flour to make a smooth batter and stir in the ground nuts.

Pour the batter into the prepared loaf pan and let stand 20 minutes. Bake in heated oven for 1¼ hours or until a skewer inserted in the center of the bread comes out clean. Let cool, then cut in slices and serve with butter.

MENU 3

TIMETABLE

Rassolnik Soup
Prepare day before but do not add sour cream. Reheat to serve, stir in sour cream off the heat and taste for seasoning. Garnish with dill pickle just before serving.

Spaghetti and Ham au Gratin
Prepare day before or in the morning and refrigerate. Bake 30–40 minutes to reheat and wrap in newspaper to keep hot if dish is to be transported.

Salads (prepare as for Menu 1)

Coffee Gelatin
Prepare in the morning and chill. About 1 hour before serving, take from refrigerator, cover with whipped cream or pastry cream and almonds. If the day is hot, chill again; if the day is cool, leave at room temperature.

Appetizer

Rassolnik Soup

3 sets of turkey or chicken giblets (without liver)
$1\frac{1}{2}$ lb shank of beef (meat only), shredded
1 tablespoon oil or meat drippings
3 medium onions, peeled
$\frac{1}{2}$ teaspoon salt
10–12 peppercorns
bouquet garni
4 quarts water
kneaded butter (made with 3 tablespoons butter and $1\frac{1}{2}$ tablespoons flour)
salt and pepper
cayenne pepper
1 cup sour cream
lemon juice (to taste)
1 large dill pickle, cut in shreds

Method
Wash the giblets, drain and cut them into medium pieces.

Heat the oil or meat drippings in a kettle, add the giblets and beef and brown over a high heat. Add the whole onions, $\frac{1}{2}$ teaspoon salt, peppercorns and bouquet garni and pour in the water. Cover and simmer $1\frac{1}{2}$–2 hours.

Strain the liquid and reserve the gizzards. Pour the liquid back into the kettle and boil to reduce to about 2 quarts. Thicken by whisking in kneaded butter a little at a time, then simmering 2 minutes. Take from heat, season with salt, pepper and cayenne, beat in the sour cream and add lemon juice to taste.

Cut 3 chicken, or 2 turkey, gizzards into thin slices, add to the soup and reheat but do not boil. Sprinkle dill pickle shreds over the top before serving.

Entrée

Spaghetti and Ham au Gratin

$1\frac{1}{2}$ lb spaghetti
$1\frac{1}{2}$ cups ($\frac{3}{4}$ lb) ham or pork luncheon meat, diced or cut into strips
$\frac{1}{2}$ cup chili sauce

For sauce
$\frac{1}{4}$ cup butter
3 tablespoons flour
2 teaspoons dry mustard, mixed to a paste with cold water
$1\frac{1}{2}$ cups water
$1\frac{1}{2}$ cups milk
salt and pepper
4 eggs, beaten to mix
$\frac{3}{4}$ cup grated Cheddar cheese

Method
Cook spaghetti in plenty of boiling salted water for 8–10 minutes or until just tender. Drain, rinse with hot water and drain again. Return spaghetti to the saucepan and cover with warm water while preparing the other ingredients.

Butter 2 shallow baking dishes and set oven at moderately hot (375°F).

Mix the ham or pork luncheon meat with chili sauce and reserve.

Melt the butter in a pan, stir in the flour and cook over low heat until straw-colored. Blend in the mustard paste, water and milk. Season with salt and pepper and cook, stirring constantly, until the mixture boils. Transfer to a bowl and cool. When cool, stir in the beaten eggs.

Drain spaghetti thoroughly and mix in the mustard sauce. Layer both spaghetti and meat mixtures in the buttered baking dishes, sprinkle the tops with grated cheese and

bake in heated oven for about 30 minutes or until set and the tops are browned.

If doubling this recipe, bake in 4 dishes.

Dessert

Coffee Gelatin

6 cups strong black coffee
3 envelopes gelatin
$\frac{1}{2}$ cup water
$\frac{3}{4}$ cup sugar
thinly peeled rind of 1 orange

For decoration
1 cup Chantilly cream (see page 69) or $1\frac{1}{2}$ cups coffee-flavored pastry cream (see page 79)
$\frac{1}{2}$ cup slivered almonds, browned

Method
In a small pan sprinkle the gelatin over the water and let stand 5 minutes or until spongy. Then dissolve over hot water.

Add the sugar and orange rind to the freshly made hot coffee and stir gently until the sugar is melted. Cover and let stand 10 minutes to let the flavor develop. Strain the coffee through a double thickness of cheesecloth to remove the orange rind. Stir in the gelatin mixture and pour into 2 glass bowls. Chill 2 hours or until set.

When set, cover the coffee gelatin with the Chantilly cream or pastry cream and sprinkle browned almonds on top.

MENU 4

Smoked Haddock Quiche

*German Potato Salad
Cole Slaw
Beet & Green Pea Salad
Carrot & Raisin Salad
Hot Herb Loaf*

*Lemon Sponge Pudding
or
Banana Cake*

TIMETABLE

Smoked Haddock Quiche
Make pastry dough and filling and bake in the morning.
If you like, reheat just before serving.

Salads (prepare as for Menu 1)

Lemon Sponge Pudding
Make sponge pudding in the morning and let set. Decorate with whipped cream and cherries about 1 hour before serving.

Banana Cake
Bake the cake 2–3 days ahead and store in an airtight container. Make and cover with frosting in the morning and keep covered.

Entrée

Smoked Haddock Quiche

For pie pastry
2 cups flour
pinch of salt
½ cup shortening
¼ cup butter
3–4 tablespoons water

For filling
2 cups cooked, flaked Finnan haddie
6–8 slices of bacon, diced
2 eggs
2 egg yolks (reserve whites for lemon sponge pudding
½ cup grated Cheddar cheese
¾ cup milk
¾ cup light cream
black pepper, freshly ground
salt (if needed)

Two 8 inch flan rings

Method
Prepare the pie pastry dough and chill it thoroughly. Divide it in half, roll out each half into a circle and line flan rings. Set oven at moderately hot (375°F).

To make the filling: in a pan fry the bacon until crisp; drain it on paper towels. In a bowl beat the whole eggs, egg yolks, cheese and milk together. Stir in the cooked, flaked Finnan haddie with the bacon and cream. Season with a little pepper, but taste the mixture before adding any salt as the fish, cheese and bacon may make the filling salty enough.

Pour the filling into the pastry-lined flan rings and bake in heated oven for about 25 minutes or until the filling is set and the top is golden brown. Serve hot or cold.
Watchpoint: it is important

that the oven is not too hot because this filling is made with eggs. To make sure the pastry on the bottom is well baked, put an extra baking sheet in the oven while it is heating, then set the filled flan rings and baking sheet on the extra baking sheet (this gives additional bottom heat).

If doubling this recipe, bake in 4 flan rings.

Accompaniments to entrée

German Potato Salad

5–6 freshly cooked potatoes, peeled and diced
6 slices of bacon, diced
2 tablespoons sugar
1 teaspoon flour
1 teaspoon salt
¼ cup vinegar
½ cup water
1 small onion, finely chopped
1 tablespoon chopped parsley

Method
Fry the bacon in a skillet until almost crisp. Pour off all but 2 tablespoons of the bacon drippings. Stir in the sugar, flour and salt until smooth. Mix the vinegar with the water, add it to the skillet and cook, stirring constantly, until the dressing comes to a boil.

Add the onion and parsley to the dressing, mix well, then add boiled potatoes while they are still hot. Taste and add more salt if needed. Let cool before serving.

For salad recipes, see pages 98–99.

Hot Herb Loaf

1 loaf French bread
½ cup butter
1 tablespoon mixed herbs (basil, tarragon, oregano)
squeeze of lemon juice
black pepper, freshly ground
½ clove of garlic, crushed (optional)

Method
Cream the butter with the herbs, lemon juice, seasoning, and garlic if used.

Cut the bread into even, slanting slices about ½ inch thick almost but not quite through the base of the loaf. Spread each slice generously with the butter mixture. Spread any remaining butter over the top and sides of the loaf and wrap in foil.

Bake in a hot oven (425°F) for 10 minutes. Reduce oven heat to 400°F, open the foil and bake the bread for 5–8 minutes longer or until it is brown and crisp.

For Menu 4 make a smoked haddock quiche, carrot and raisin salad, cole slaw, German potato salad, and a lemon sponge pudding

Dessert

Lemon Sponge Pudding

4 lemons
$\frac{1}{2}-\frac{3}{4}$ cup sugar
2 cups water
2 envelopes gelatin
4 egg whites
2 tablespoons sherry

For decoration
1 cup heavy cream, stiffly
   whipped
several candied cherries

Pastry bag and star tube

Method
With a vegetable peeler, thinly peel the rind from the lemons. Put the rind in a saucepan with the sugar and water, sprinkle over the gelatin and infuse over a very low heat for 8–10 minutes, stirring occasionally, until the sugar and gelatin have dissolved. Strain the mixture and cool.

Cut the lemons in half, squeeze to remove the juice and strain into the cool gelatin mixture. When this starts to set, add the egg whites and sherry and beat with an electric or rotary beater until the mixture is white and frothy. Pour it into a glass bowl and refrigerate.

If the mixture starts to separate, beat it again when it is almost set. Chill several hours until firm.

Fill the pastry bag, fitted with a star tube, with the stiffly whipped cream and decorate the top of the pudding with cream and candied cherries.

If you want to double this recipe, make as 2 separate puddings.

Alternative dessert

Banana Cake

$1\frac{1}{2}$ cups mashed ripe bananas
   (about 3 bananas)
2 cups cake flour
$1\frac{1}{2}$ cups sugar
$2\frac{1}{2}$ teaspoons baking powder
$\frac{1}{2}$ teaspoon baking soda
$\frac{1}{2}$ teaspoon salt
$\frac{1}{2}$ cup butter
2 eggs
1 teaspoon vanilla

For banana frosting
2 bananas
$\frac{1}{3}$ cup butter
6 cups confectioners' sugar
pinch of salt
juice of $\frac{1}{2}$ lemon

9 inch springform pan

Method
Set the oven at moderate (350°F); grease the cake pan.

Sift the flour, sugar, baking powder, baking soda and salt into a bowl. Add the butter, $\frac{1}{2}$ cup of the mashed bananas and the unbeaten eggs. Beat 2–3 minutes until the batter is very smooth. Add the remaining mashed banana and vanilla and beat 1 minute longer.

Spoon the batter into the prepared cake pan and bake in heated oven for 1 hour or until a skewer inserted in the center of the cake comes out clean. Transfer the cake to a wire rack to cool.

To make the banana frosting: cream the butter, gradually beat in the confectioners' sugar and continue beating until the mixture is quite soft. Stir in the mashed bananas, salt and lemon juice. If the frosting is very soft, add more sugar.

Split the cake, sandwich it with half the frosting and spread the remaining frosting on top.

The menus on pages 98–105 serve 8 people. Many of the recipes can be doubled or tripled without difficulty. However, to avoid the problems involved in large-scale cooking, we suggest you ask other people to cook 1–2 dishes each and, with very little effort, you can provide enough food for 24 people or even more.

FRENCH COUNTRY COOKING

Country cooking in France does not just mean regional specialties; there is a distinct culinary style known as 'bourgeoise', meaning simple, honest dishes in which top quality ingredients are cooked in ways that best develop their flavors. This is the everyday fare of France, appreciated as much as the elaborate recipes of haute cuisine that are reserved for special occasions, and even preferred to them. Obvious examples of French country cooking are hearty recipes like French onion soup or boeuf bourguignon stew, but 'la bonne cuisine bougeoise' also includes simple fare like veal escalopes fried to perfection in butter or a creamy purée of mashed potatoes.

Soupe à l'oignon (onion soup) is one of the most famous of all French recipes

Soupe à l'Oignon 1
(French Onion Soup)

5–6 yellow onions, thinly
   sliced or chopped
$\frac{1}{4}$ cup butter
6 cups stock
salt and pepper
$\frac{1}{2}$–1 cup Champagne (optional)

To finish
4–6 slices of French bread
$\frac{3}{4}$ cup grated Parmesan cheese
$\frac{3}{4}$ cup grated Gruyère cheese
1 egg per person (for onion
   soup version 1)
1 egg yolk and 1 tablespoon
   port per person (for onion
   soup version 2)

*4–6 individual heatproof soup
   pots (marmites)*

Soupe à l'oignon is one of the
most famous of all French
recipes. The best onion soup
is made with meat or vegetable stock and a glass of
Champagne may be added,
if you like.

There are many versions;
we give two of them here.
Serves 4–6 people.

Method
In a kettle melt the butter and
fry the onion very gently until
a deep golden brown; do not
let them scorch. In another
pan bring the stock to a boil,
add to the onion, season,
cover and simmer 15 minutes,
then add Champagne, if used.

To finish onion soup version
1: sprinkle the slices of bread
with a little grated Parmesan
and Gruyère cheese, mixed,
and put a slice into each soup
pot. Pour over the boiling
soup, put the lids on the pots
and serve a small dish of the
remaining cheese and a fresh
egg with each pot. Each guest
breaks the raw egg into the
soup, adds the cheese and

beats it in with a fork. The
soup must be very hot so that
the egg cooks a little and
thickens the broth slightly.

Soupe à l'Oignon 2

Make the onion soup as for
the previous recipe, but to
finish, bake the slices of bread
in a low oven (300°F) until dry
and lightly browned; set a
slice in each pot. Pour over
the soup and sprinkle each
bowl with the grated
Parmesan and Gruyère
cheese, mixed.

Put the pots of soup under
the broiler until the cheese
browns. Mix each egg yolk
with 1 tablespoon port, lift
up the side of the browned
topping, and pour the mixture
into the soup. Serve at once.

*To finish French onion soup
version 1, sprinkle the slices
of bread with grated cheese
and put a slice into each
marmite pot. Pour over the
boiling soup, put on the lids
and serve very hot.*

Garbure Paysanne

1 medium white turnip, thinly
   sliced
2 medium carrots, thinly sliced
$\frac{1}{2}$ small head of cabbage, thinly
   sliced
2 medium onions, thinly sliced
white part of 2 leeks, thinly
   sliced
5–6 stalks of celery, thinly
   sliced
2 medium potatoes, thinly
   sliced
3 tablespoons butter
$\frac{1}{3}$ cup dried navy or Great
   Northern beans, soaked
   overnight and cooked
salt and pepper
2–2$\frac{1}{2}$ quarts water or stock
1 long crusty roll, cut in slices
   and fried in 2–3 tablespoons
   butter (for croûtes)
$\frac{1}{4}$–$\frac{1}{2}$ cup grated Gruyère cheese
2 tablespoons butter (to finish)
   – optional

This peasant soup is so substantial that it is often eaten
as a main dish. The garnish of
croûtes is characteristic; in
some parts of France they are
browned in butter, in others
they are baked in the oven.

Method
In a large heavy-based kettle
or flameproof casserole melt
2 tablespoons butter and add
the turnip, carrot, cabbage,
onion, leek, celery and potato.
Press a piece of buttered foil
on top, add the lid and cook
very gently (sweat) for 15–20
minutes or until the vegetables are fairly tender; do not
let them brown. Add the
beans, a little seasoning and
5 cups water or stock or
enough to cover the vege-
tables well. Cover and simmer 20–30 minutes or until
the vegetables are very
tender.

Fry the croûtes and drain
on paper towels.

Lift about 2 tablespoons
vegetables from the soup
with a slotted spoon and work
them through a sieve. Put
them in a small pan with the
remaining tablespoon of
butter and cook, stirring, to
the consistency of mashed
potato. Spread this purée
over the croûtes, doming it
well, and sprinkle with grated
cheese. Bake the croûtes in
a moderately hot oven
(375°F) for 10–12 minutes
or until browned.

Work the remaining soup
through a sieve or purée in a
blender; add the remaining
water or stock and simmer
10–15 minutes longer or until
the soup is smooth and the
thickness of light cream.
Season well and, if you like,
stir in 2 tablespoons butter in
small pieces.

Serve the soup very hot
with the croûtes floating in
each bowl or serve them
separately.

Brandade de Morue
(Mousse of Salt Cod)

1½ lb shredded salt cod
1 cup heavy cream
1 cup olive oil
1 clove of garlic, bruised
black pepper, freshly ground
pinch of grated nutmeg

For serving
3–4 slices of bread, crusts removed, cut in triangles and fried in 3–4 tablespoons oil and butter, mixed (for croûtes)
½ cup ripe or green Italian-style olives, pitted (optional)

Salt cod is a Mediterranean staple and this dish, in which the fish is pounded with cream and olive oil to a smooth mousse, is a specialty of Languedoc and Provence. Serves 4–6 people.

Method
Soak the shredded salt cod for about 5 hours in several changes of water. Drain, set in a baking dish, cover with cold water and a sheet of foil and bake in a moderate oven (350°F) for 20–25 minutes or until tender; drain thoroughly. Work it several times through the fine blade of a grinder or pound in a mortar and pestle until smooth.
Watchpoint: it is essential to break down the fibers of the fish so it will absorb the oil and cream.

Scald the cream and keep hot. In a skillet heat the oil, fry the garlic until golden, then discard it.

Put the fish purée in a saucepan, add about 2 tablespoons hot cream and beat over very low heat until the cream is absorbed. Add 2 tablespoons hot oil and continue beating, adding the cream and oil alternately in small amounts until all is added and the mixture is as light and fluffy as mashed potatoes. Season with pepper and a little nutmeg.

Pile brandade in a mound on a platter and surround with the croûtes and olives, if you like.

Matelote de Poisson
(Fish Stew with White Wine)

¾ lb salmon steaks
¾ lb halibut steaks
½ lb sea scallops, cut in 2–3 even-sized pieces
1½ cups white wine
salt and pepper
6 tablespoons butter

For court bouillon
2 medium carrots, sliced
2 medium onions, sliced
1 leek, sliced (optional)
bouquet garni
stalk of celery, sliced
blade of mace
1 quart water

For sauce
3 tablespoons butter
2 tablespoons flour
1 cup mushrooms, trimmed
squeeze of lemon juice
2 egg yolks
1 cup heavy cream

A mixture of almost any fish can be used for this stew — cod, haddock and sea bass are particularly suitable. Cooked lobster meat and shrimps can be added to the cooked fish mixture before the sauce is poured over.

Method
Put all the ingredients for the court bouillon in a kettle, cover and simmer 30 minutes, strain and reserve.

Cut the salmon and halibut steaks into large pieces, discarding the skin and bones. Arrange the fish in layers in a flameproof casserole, first the salmon, then the halibut, then the scallops. Pour over the court bouillon, add the wine and seasoning, and poach, uncovered, for 15 minutes.

To make the sauce: melt the butter in a saucepan, stir in the flour and cook until straw-colored. Take from the heat and carefully pour in all the cooking liquid from the fish, tilting the pot so the fish is not disturbed. Bring the sauce to a boil, stirring, and simmer 10–15 minutes or until it is well reduced and slightly thickened.

Add the mushrooms and a squeeze of lemon juice to the sauce and simmer 1–2 minutes longer until the mushrooms are tender. Mix the egg yolks with the cream, stir in a little of the hot sauce and stir this liaison back into the remaining sauce. Heat gently, stirring, until the sauce thickens slightly, but do not boil or it will curdle. Taste for seasoning, pour over the fish and warm 1–2 minutes over very low heat. Serve in the pot with buttered noodles.

> **Matelote** (or sailor-style) is the French name for a fish stew made with wine. The same name is also sometimes given to dishes made with veal and poultry.

Matelote Mâconnaise
(Fish Stew with Red Wine)

about 2 lb mixed fish
¼ cup butter
1 onion, finely chopped
1 cup Burgundy or other red wine
1½ cups fish stock
bouquet garni
salt and pepper
18–20 small onions, blanched and peeled
12–14 small mushrooms, trimmed
kneaded butter (made with 2 tablespoons butter and 1 tablespoon flour)
1 tablespoon chopped parsley
3–4 slices of bread, crusts removed, cut in triangles and fried in 3–4 tablespoons oil and butter, mixed (for croûtes)

This version uses red wine from Mâcon in Burgundy. Traditionally, it is made with freshwater fish such as pike, eel, catfish and lake whitefish. However, sea fish like cod, haddock, halibut, mackerel, bass and red snapper can also be used. The more types of fish that are included, the better the stew will taste.

Method
Cut the fish into chunks, discarding the skin and as much bone as possible. Melt 2 tablespoons butter in a shallow flameproof casserole, add the chopped onion and fish and cook over low heat until golden· brown on all sides. Add the wine, bring quickly to a boil and flame. Simmer until reduced by half, then add the stock, bouquet garni and seasoning and simmer gently for 5 minutes.

In a frying pan heat 2 more tablespoons butter and fry the

Matelote mâconnaise, made with freshwater and sea fish, is garnished with croûtes and parsley

small, whole onions over low heat until golden brown and tender. Add the mushrooms and continue cooking until tender also.

Discard the bouquet garni from the fish, add the onions and mushrooms and thicken the sauce by adding the kneaded butter in small pieces and shaking the pan over the heat until the butter melts and thickens the sauce. Simmer 2–3 minutes longer or until the fish flakes easily. Taste for seasoning.

Pile the fish in the center of a serving dish, spoon over the sauce, sprinkle with chopped parsley and surround the dish with the croûtes. Serve with boiled potatoes.

Fish Stock

Blanch 1 large onion, peeled and sliced; drain and refresh. Melt 1 tablespoon butter in a large saucepan, add onion and 1 lb washed fish bones, cover and cook slowly for 5 minutes. Add 1 carrot, peeled and sliced, 1 stalk celery, sliced, 6 cups water, bouquet garni, $\frac{1}{2}$ teaspoon salt, 6 peppercorns, $\frac{1}{2}$ cup dry white wine and a slice of lemon. Simmer gently, uncovered, for 20 minutes; strain and measure. Makes about 5 cups.

Baked stuffed mussels are served in the half shell

Baked Stuffed Mussels

3 quarts mussels
1 cup white wine

For stuffing
1 onion, finely chopped
$\frac{1}{4}$ cup butter
$\frac{1}{2}$ cup fresh white breadcrumbs
1–2 cloves of garlic, crushed
2 tablespoons chopped parsley
1 tablespoon chopped fresh dill
    (optional)
salt
black pepper, freshly ground

*Shallow baking dish or 4
    individual gratin dishes*

Method

Wash the mussels thoroughly and scrub them to remove any weed; discard mussels that do not close when tapped or have broken shells.

Put the mussels in a kettle with the wine, cover and cook over high heat for 5–7 minutes or until the shells open, stirring once. Let mussels cool, then discard the top shells and 'beard' (the gristly ring around the edge of the shell). Discard any mussels that have not opened. Strain the cooking liquid through cheesecloth and reserve it.

To make the stuffing: fry the onion in the butter until soft. Add the onion to the breadcrumbs with the garlic, herbs and seasoning, and enough reserved cooking liquid to bind the mixture together.

Put 1 teaspoon stuffing on each mussel in the half shell and set them in the baking dish or gratin dishes. Sprinkle over the remaining cooking liquid and bake in a hot oven (400°F) for 15 minutes or until very hot and brown.

Bouillabaisse
(Mediterranean Fish Stew)

3 lb white fish such as red
    snapper, perch, haddock,
    porgy, flounder and cod
2 lb rich fish such as eel,
    Spanish mackerel, or striped
    bass
1 lb unpeeled, uncooked
    shrimps
8–10 small spiny lobster tails,
    or 8–10 small blue crabs
$\frac{3}{4}$ cup olive oil
2 medium onions, chopped
white part of 2 leeks, sliced,
    or 1 more onion, chopped
3 ripe tomatoes, peeled, seeded
    and chopped
3–5 cloves of garlic, crushed
bouquet garni
thinly peeled strip of orange
    rind
2 sprigs of fresh fennel or
    1 teaspoon dried fennel
salt and pepper
$\frac{1}{4}$ teaspoon saffron
3–4 quarts boiling water
1 long loaf of French bread, cut
    into about 20 slices
$\frac{1}{4}$ cup chopped parsley

Bouillabaisse fish stew is a specialty of the French Mediterranean coast and true bouillabaisse must be made with Mediterranean fish. However, an excellent imitation can be made with fish available here and the greater the variety used, the better the bouillabaisse will be.

The secret of a good bouillabaisse is to use fresh fish and cook it quickly. This way the large amount of oil used is emulsified in the broth and does not float on the surface. A mixture of white and rich fleshed fish should be used as well as shellfish like shrimps, spiny lobster (rock lobster) and crabs. Because a large variety of fish must be included, it is hard to make bouillabaisse for less than 8 people.

Bouillabaisse is served in 2 dishes, one for the pieces of fish, the other (a bowl or soup tureen) containing slices of French bread with the broth poured on top. It must be served very hot. Serves 8–10 people.

Method

Cut the fish in chunks, discarding the skin and as many bones as possible; leave all shellfish in the shells.

In a very large kettle or flameproof casserole put the oil with the onion and leeks, if used, and cook 1 minute without browning. Add the tomato, garlic, bouquet garni, orange rind and fennel and lay first the shellfish on top, then the rich fish. Season, sprinkle in the saffron and pour on enough boiling water to cover the fish. Bring to a boil, uncovered, as quickly as possible and boil hard for 5–7 minutes; do not stir but shake the pan gently from time to time to prevent the mixture from sticking.

Put the white fish on top and boil 5 minutes longer – the total cooking time must not be more than 15 minutes. Be sure that the fast-boiling liquid covers all the pieces of fish – if not add a little more boiling water.

Put the bread in the bottom of a soup tureen or large bowl. Take the pan from the heat and transfer the fish as quickly as possible to a hot deep platter, using a slotted spoon, and arranging the fish so the different kinds are separated. Keep it warm.

Strain three-quarters of the fish broth over the bread and let stand 1–2 minutes or until the bread is swollen. If all the broth has been absorbed, add the remaining broth – the soup should be thick but not solid with bread. Sprinkle both dishes with chopped parsley and serve at once.

Tripes à la Mode de Caen
(Braised Tripe with White Wine and Apple Brandy)

1½–2 lb fresh tripe
1 carrot, diced
1 onion, diced
1 stalk of celery, diced
1 calf's foot, boned and cut in small pieces
bouquet garni
2 whole cloves
½ teaspoon whole allspice
salt and pepper
1 cup white wine
¼ cup Calvados or other apple brandy
stock (see method)
¼ lb salt pork, thinly sliced
luting paste (see box, right)

The favorite way of cooking tripe in France is to braise it very slowly 'à la mode de Caen' with white wine and an apple brandy called Calvados. The town of Caen lies at the edge of the Calvados region of Normandy in northern France. A mixture of all 4 kinds of tripe – the fat part (called 'gras double' in France), and the honeycomb sections should be used for this dish.

Method
Trim the tripe, wash thoroughly and soak overnight in cold water. Drain, blanch in salted water for 15 minutes. Drain, rinse and cut into 2–3 inch squares.

In a flameproof casserole spread the carrot, onion and celery and place the tripe on top with the pieces of calf's foot. Add the bouquet garni, cloves, allspice and seasoning, pour over the wine and apple brandy and enough stock just to cover the tripe. Lay the slices of salt pork on top (this moistens the tripe

during cooking) and add the lid. Seal the space between the lid and casserole with luting paste and bake the tripe in a low oven (275°F) for 9–12 hours or overnight.

To serve, lift out the pieces of tripe, arrange them in a serving dish and keep warm. Strain the sauce, skim off the fat from the surface with a metal spoon and taste for seasoning. Spoon the sauce over the tripe and serve with mashed potatoes.

Luting paste is a flour and water mixture used to seal terrines and casseroles. To make it, stir 6–7 tablespoons water into 1 cup flour with a teaspoon or your forefinger to form a paste. Do not stir too much or the paste will become elastic and shrink during cooking. Spread with the fingers, pressing well into the gap between the casserole and lid.

Petite Marmite
(Chicken, Meat and Vegetable Stew)

3–3½ lb roasting chicken, with giblets
2 lb round roast of beef
2 lb veal shank, cut in 2–3 inch slices
about 3 quarts water
2 teaspoons salt
2 large carrots, quartered
2–3 onions, 1 stuck with a clove
2–3 stalks of celery, cut in 2 inch lengths
4–6 small white turnips
bouquet garni
6 peppercorns

For garnish
½ small head of cabbage, shredded
1 medium white turnip, cut in julienne strips
1 leek, cut in julienne strips (optional)
1 carrot, cut in julienne strips
2–3 long hard rolls, cut in ½ inch slices (for croûtes)

Petite marmite is like pot-au-feu (see Volume 1), the French version of boiled beef. A marmite is the heatproof soup pot in which it is cooked. Petite marmite is flavored with chicken as well as beef and veal. The chicken and meat are simmered with vegetables, then the broth is strained to serve as soup, with the stew as the entrée. Toasted or baked croûtes of bread and julienne strips of vegetable are often added to the soup as garnish. Serves 6 people.

Method
Put the beef and veal in a large kettle with water to cover and salt. Bring slowly to a boil, uncovered, skimming as the scum rises to the surface. When the mixture

comes to a boil, add ¼ cup cold water and skim. Repeat this process once; adding cold water helps to clear the liquid. Simmer 1 hour, then add the chicken and giblets (not liver), vegetables, bouquet garni and peppercorns. Skim again, if necessary, and partially cover the pan with the lid. Simmer ¾–1 hour longer or until the meat and chicken are tender.

To prepare the garnish: blanch the cabbage in boiling salted water for 1 minute, drain, refresh and drain well. Cook the turnip, leek, if used, and carrot strips in boiling salted water for 5 minutes or until tender and drain them.

Skim the fat from the surface of the broth and spoon a little over the slices of bread in a baking dish. Bake in a moderate oven (350°F) for 10–15 minutes or until the bread is crisp, then place the slices in soup bowls.

When cooked, lift out the chicken, beef, veal and vegetables and boil remaining broth 10–15 minutes or until well reduced. Arrange the vegetables and veal shanks on a platter. Slice the beef, carve the legs and wings from the chicken, arrange on the platter and keep warm. Cut the chicken breasts into thin strips.

When the broth is well flavored, discard the bouquet garni and peppercorns, add the vegetables for garnish and the chicken strips. Bring just to a boil, taste for seasoning and pour over the croûtes of bread in bowls. Serve the soup, followed by the boiled meat, chicken and vegetables.

Poulet au Riz
(Chicken with Rice)

3½–4 lb roasting chicken or fowl
1 onion, quartered
1 carrot, quartered
bouquet garni
6 peppercorns
salt
1½ quarts water
2½ cups chicken stock (see method)
1 cup rice
pepper
¼ cup butter
2 cups (½ lb) small mushrooms
velouté sauce (made with 1½ tablespoons butter, 1½ tablespoons flour, 1½ cups chicken stock) – see method
2 egg yolks, ¼ cup heavy cream (for liaison)
squeeze of lemon juice

This is a favorite French way of using an old fowl – the bird can be simmered long enough to be completely tender and adds more flavor to the sauce than a young chicken.

Method
Put the chicken or fowl in a large kettle with the onion, carrot, bouquet garni, peppercorns, a little salt and the water. Cover and simmer ¾–1 hour for the chicken, or about 1½ hours for the fowl, or until the bird is tender and no pink juice runs out when the thigh is pierced with a skewer.

Twenty minutes before the end of cooking, strain off 2½ cups stock from the pan. Put the uncooked rice with the strained stock in a pan, add seasoning, cover and simmer 15–18 minutes or until all the stock is absorbed and the rice is just tender. Dot the surface of the rice with 2 tablespoons of the butter, cover and keep warm.

Melt the remaining butter in a skillet and sauté the mush-rooms gently for 1–2 minutes or until tender, season and keep warm.

When the bird is cooked, strain off the stock and leave the bird in the pan to keep warm. Make the velouté sauce, using 1½ cups of the strained stock. Simmer 4–5 minutes or until the sauce is the consistency of heavy cream. Add a little of the sauce to the liaison of egg yolks and cream, stir mixture into remaining sauce, heat gently and stir until the sauce thickens slightly but do not let it boil. Take from the heat, add the lemon juice and taste for seasoning.

Carve the bird, arrange the pieces on a platter and coat them with sauce. Stir the rice with a fork to separate the grains, spoon it down one side of the platter and arrange the mushrooms down the other side. Serve the remaining sauce separately.

To Make Chop Frills

Fold a 10 X 3 inch sheet of plain white paper in half lengthwise. With scissors make a series of even cuts ⅛ inch apart to within ¾ inch of the unfolded long edges and turn the paper inside out so the cut part is looped. Stick the two long edges together with glue and cut to make 4 frills. Fold each in a circle and attach the ends to complete the chop frill.

Poulet au Romarin
(Roast Chicken with Rosemary)

3 broiling chickens (2–2½ lb each)
4–5 sprigs of fresh rosemary
¼ cup butter
½ cup white wine
1 cup chicken stock
salt and pepper
1 cup heavy cream
1 teaspoon arrowroot mixed to a paste with 1 tablespoon water

Trussing needle and string

Method
Put a sprig of rosemary inside each chicken and truss them. In a large flameproof cas-serole melt the butter and brown the chickens on all sides. Set them on one side, add the wine, half the stock, the remaining rosemary leaves, stripped from the stems, and seasoning, and cover the pan. Cook gently on top of the stove or in a moderately hot oven (375°F) for 30–40 minutes or until the chickens are tender and no pink juice runs out when the thighs are pricked with a skewer. Turn them from one side to the other, then onto their backs during cooking.

Remove the trussing strings transfer the chickens to a platter and keep warm.

Add the stock to the cook-ing juices, bring to a boil and work through a sieve to purée the rosemary leaves or purée in a blender. Return the sauce to a pan, add the cream and bring just to a boil; stir in the arrowroot paste until the sauce thickens slightly. Taste for seasoning, spoon a little sauce around the chickens and serve the rest separately. Decorate the legs of the chickens with chop frills, if you like. Serves 6.

Chicken Marengo is garnished with crayfish tails and fried eggs on croûtes of bread dipped in sauce and chopped parsley

Poulet Marengo
(Chicken Marengo)

3½–4 lb roasting chicken, cut
  in pieces
1 tablespoon oil
2 tablespoons butter
2 tomatoes, peeled, seeded
  and chopped
1 clove of garlic, crushed
1 tablespoon tomato paste
½ cup white wine
1½ cups espagnole sauce
  (see Volume 2)
2 cups (½ lb) mushrooms,
  trimmed

For garnish
4 crayfish tails or 4 large
  shrimps
2 tablespoons stock or water
1 tablespoon chopped parsley
4 slices of bread, cut into
  heart-shapes and fried in
  3–4 tablespoons butter
  (for croûtes)
4 small eggs

Method

In a shallow flameproof casserole or skillet heat the oil
and butter and brown the
chicken pieces on all sides.
Remove them; drain and
reserve the fat from the pan.
Add the chopped tomato,
garlic and tomato paste to the
pan and cook gently, stirring,
for 2–3 minutes. Add the wine
and boil until reduced by half.
Pour in the espagnole sauce,
replace the chicken, add the
mushrooms, cover and sim-
mer 30–35 minutes or until
the chicken is very tender.

To prepare the garnish:
simmer the crayfish tails or
shrimps in the stock or salted
water for 3–4 minutes or until
tender; drain and keep warm.

Arrange the chicken on a
platter and spoon over the
sauce. Dip the point of each
croûte in the sauce, then into
chopped parsley and arrange
the croûtes around the edge
of the platter with the cray-

fish tails or shrimps and keep
warm.

Heat the reserved fat from
the pan and fry the eggs. Set
an egg on each croûte and
serve at once.

Chicken Marengo was
hastily composed by
Napoleon's chef on the
night of June 14, 1800,
when the Austrians were
defeated at the Battle of
Marengo. All that could
be found for the celebra-
tion was a small hen and
eggs, tomatoes, crayfish
and garlic – but the result
has become a classic dish.

Ragoût de Dinde à la Bourgeoise
(Ragoût of Turkey with Vegetables)

5–6 lb turkey
2 tablespoons oil
2 tablespoons butter
1 large onion, cut in wedges
1 large carrot, thickly sliced
1½ tablespoons flour
2 cups stock
½ cup white wine
bouquet garni
1 clove of garlic, crushed
salt and pepper

For garnish
½ lb piece of lean bacon, diced
16–18 baby onions, blanched
  and peeled
8–10 carrots, cut in 2 inch
  lengths and trimmed to ovals
1 tablespoon chopped parsley

'A la bourgeoise' always refers
to a garnish of diced bacon,
baby onions and carrots cut to
a uniform size. Serves 6
people.

Method

Cut the turkey into 8 pieces
as for a chicken, discarding
backbone and dividing the
breast in half.

In a flameproof casserole
heat the oil and butter and
brown the turkey pieces on all
sides. Take out, add the onion
wedges and sliced carrot and
brown also. Sprinkle in the
flour and cook, stirring, until
well browned, then pour in the
stock and wine. Add the bouquet garni, garlic and seasoning, bring to a boil and replace
turkey pieces; half cover the
pan and simmer 30–35 min-
utes.

To prepare the garnish: in
another flameproof casserole
fry the diced bacon until
browned, add the baby onions
and carrots and sauté gently
until lightly browned.

Lift out the turkey pieces
and place on top of the vegetables for the garnish. Taste
the sauce in the pan for
seasoning and strain over the
turkey. Cover the casserole
and bake in a moderate oven
(350°F) for 20–30 minutes or
until the turkey and vegetables
are tender.

Serve the turkey in the
casserole or transfer to a platter and spoon the sauce and
vegetables on top. Serve with
braised celery and buttered
new potatoes tossed in chopped parsley.

Braised Celery

bunch of celery
1 large onion, diced
1 large carrot, diced
2 tablespoons butter
1 cup jellied stock
salt and pepper
bouquet garni

Method

Wash celery and slice off
some of the leaves. Split the
bunch in four and blanch in
boiling salted water; drain.

In a large flameproof casserole sweat the onion and
carrot in butter by covering
tightly with foil and the lid and
cooking over very low heat
until the vegetables are soft
but not browned.

Put the celery, stock, salt,
pepper and bouquet garni in
with the vegetables. Cover
and braise for 1–1½ hours or
until tender in a moderately
low oven (325°F), basting
from time to time. When
cooked, the sauce should be
well reduced and the celery
glazed. Strain the sauce and
pour over the celery in a vegetable dish.

Pigeons en Cocotte Normande
(Casserole of Squabs with Apple Rings)

4 squabs
2 tablespoons butter
1 medium onion, sliced
1 medium-sized tart apple
1 tablespoon flour
$\frac{3}{4}$ cup stock
$\frac{1}{2}$ cup cider
salt and pepper
bouquet garni

For garnish
2 medium-sized tart apples
8 slices of bacon
1 tablespoon chopped parsley

Trussing needle and string

Method
Set oven at moderate (350°F); truss the squabs.

In a flameproof casserole heat the butter and brown the birds slowly on all sides. Take them from the pan and cut them in half, discarding the backbones. Add the onion to the pan and cook until golden brown.

Wipe, quarter, core and slice 1 apple and add to the pan with the browned onion. Increase the heat to high and brown the apple also. Sprinkle in the flour, cook quickly until lightly browned, then pour in the stock and cider. Bring to a boil, season, add the bouquet garni and the squabs. Cover the casserole tightly and bake in heated oven for 25–30 minutes or until the squabs are tender. Arrange them, overlapping, on a platter and keep warm.

Strain the sauce and, if necessary, boil it until reduced to the consistency of light cream. Taste for seasoning and spoon over squabs.

To prepare the garnish: wipe the apples, core them and cut them in rings, $\frac{1}{2}$ inch thick. Fry the bacon until crisp and drain on paper towels. Fry the apple rings in the bacon fat over medium heat until they are browned on both sides and just tender.

Arrange the apple rings, overlapping, around squabs, put bacon slices on top and sprinkle the dish with parsley. Serve with sautéed potatoes.

Poitrine de Veau Braisé Farci
(Braised Stuffed Breast of Veal)

$3\frac{1}{2}$–4 lb breast of veal, boned but not rolled
2 veal kidneys
2 tablespoons butter
$\frac{1}{4}$ lb piece of bacon, diced
2 carrots, sliced
1 onion, sliced
$1\frac{1}{2}$–2 cups stock
bouquet garni
salt and pepper
1 teaspoon arrowroot mixed to a paste with 1 tablespoon water

For stuffing
2 shallots or 1 small onion, chopped
2 tablespoons butter
1 lb loose pork sausage meat
1 tablespoon chopped parsley
1 teaspoon mixed herbs – oregano and thyme

Trussing needle and string

The virtues of breast of veal have long been appreciated in France, but this cut has only recently become popular here. The best way to serve it is boned and rolled with stuffing.

Method
Remove the skin from the kidneys if not already done and cut out the core with scissors, leaving each kidney in one piece.

To make the stuffing: cook the shallot or onion in the butter until soft but not browned; stir into the sausage meat with the herbs and plenty of seasoning.

Spread the stuffing over the cut surface of the veal and put the kidneys in the center. Roll up the meat, sew with string and tie at 2 inch intervals to make a neat roll.

In a flameproof casserole heat the butter and brown the veal slowly on all sides. Take from the pot, add the bacon and cook slowly until beginning to brown. Drain off all but 2 tablespoons fat, add the carrots and onion, cover the pot and cook gently for 5–7 minutes or until all the fat is absorbed.

Replace the veal on the vegetables, pour on $1\frac{1}{2}$ cups stock, add the bouquet garni and seasoning, cover with foil, add the lid and braise in a moderately low oven (325°F) for 2–$2\frac{1}{2}$ hours or until the meat is very tender when pierced with a skewer. Add more stock during cooking if the liquid evaporates quickly.

Take out the meat and keep warm. Strain the cooking liquid into a saucepan, pressing the vegetables well to extract the juice. Bring the liquid to a boil, stir in the arrowroot paste until the sauce thickens, take from the heat and taste for seasoning.

Remove the strings from the veal, carve several slices from the meat and arrange on a platter. Spoon over a little of the sauce and serve the rest separately. Endive ardennaise is a good accompaniment (see page 122).

Filet de Porc Farci Lyonnaise
(Stuffed Pork Tenderloin with Onion and Celery Fondue)

2 (about 1 lb each) pork tenderloins
2 tablespoons butter
3 mild or Bermuda onions, sliced
small bunch of celery, sliced
about $\frac{3}{4}$ cup stock
$\frac{1}{2}$ cup heavy cream
1 teaspoon arrowroot, mixed to a paste with 1 tablespoon water (for liaison)

For stuffing
$\frac{1}{2}$ lb ground pork
1 medium onion, finely chopped
2 tablespoons butter
$\frac{3}{4}$ cup fresh white breadcrumbs
1 teaspoon sage
1 tablespoon chopped parsley
salt and pepper
1 egg yolk

Trussing needle and string (optional)

Method
To make the stuffing: fry the onion in the butter until soft but not browned. Add to the ground pork with the breadcrumbs, herbs and seasoning. Mix well and stir in the egg yolk to bind the mixture.

Make a slit down the length of each tenderloin and open the meat so it is flat. Lay each tenderloin between 2 sheets of wax paper and pound with a rolling pin or mallet to flatten slightly.

Spread the stuffing on one tenderloin and cover with the other, arranging neatly head to tail. Roll slightly to neaten the shape and sew up with a trussing needle and string or tie with string.

Set oven at moderate

(350°F).

In a flameproof casserole heat the butter and brown the pork on all sides. Remove the pork, add the onions and celery and cook 6–7 minutes until the fat is absorbed, stirring frequently. Replace the pork on top, pour around the stock, cover the pot tightly and braise in the heated oven for 40–50 minutes or until the pork is tender.

Take out the pork, lift out the onion and celery with a slotted spoon and arrange down the center of a platter. Remove the strings from the pork, carve it in $\frac{1}{2}$ inch slices and arrange on top of the vegetable fondue.

Add the cream to the cooking juices in the pot, bring to a boil and stir in the arrowroot paste until the sauce thickens. Spoon the sauce around the pork and serve with mashed potatoes.

Place other tenderloin on top, head to tail; sew up or tie with string

Côtes de Porc Ardennaise
(Pork Chops with Ham)

4 thick or 8 thin loin pork chops
½ lb cooked ham, diced or cut into strips
3 shallots, finely chopped
1 cup white wine
¼ cup seasoned flour (made with ¼ teaspoon salt and pinch of pepper)
¼ cup butter
1 cup heavy cream
1 teaspoon Dijon-style mustard
salt and pepper
black pepper, freshly ground
1 tablespoon chopped parsley

This recipe and the one for endive ardennaise (see page 122) are named for the Belgian region of the Ardennes, famous for its ham.

Method
Put the ham, shallots and wine in a bowl; cover and let marinate 30 minutes. Drain and reserve wine, keeping the ham and shallots separately.

Coat the chops in the seasoned flour. In a frying pan or skillet heat the butter and gently fry the chops for 4–5 minutes on each side or until browned. Add the shallots and ham and cook 2–3 minutes longer. Pour in the reserved wine and simmer 2–3 minutes for thinly cut chops, 10–12 minutes for thick chops, or until they are very tender. Take them out and arrange, overlapping, on a warm platter.

Boil the sauce, if necessary, to reduce to ½ cup, stir in the cream and bring to a boil. Take from the heat, stir in the mustard, taste for seasoning and spoon the sauce over the chops. Sprinkle with parsley before serving with boiled potatoes.

Lapin Dijonnaise
(Rabbit in Mustard Sauce)

4–6 pieces of rabbit
1 teaspoon vinegar (optional)
salt
½ lb piece of bacon or salt pork, diced
2 tablespoons bacon fat or drippings
4 medium onions, quartered
1 tablespoon flour
2–2½ cups stock
bouquet garni
black pepper, freshly ground
½ cup heavy cream
1 tablespoon Dijon-style mustard
1 tablespoon chopped parsley (for garnish)

One of the favorite Sunday sports of the French countryman used to be hunting rabbits but disease has killed so many that most French cooks now are forced to use domestic rabbits, that have a milder flavor. This recipe can also be made with chicken pieces.

Method
If using wild rabbit, soak the pieces overnight in water to cover with the vinegar and 1 teaspoon salt. Drain and dry them on paper towels. Domestic rabbit needs no soaking.

Blanch the bacon or salt pork in boiling salted water for 15 minutes and drain.

In a flameproof casserole heat the bacon fat or drippings and brown the rabbit pieces on all sides. Take out, add the bacon or salt pork and brown it. Take out, add the onions and brown them also. Stir in the flour, cook 1–2 minutes until it is beginning to brown and pour in 2 cups stock.

Put back the rabbit pieces, bacon or salt pork and add the bouquet garni and some black pepper. Salt will not be needed if the bacon or salt pork was salty.

Cover the pot and cook in a moderate oven (350°F) for 1–1½ hours or until the meat is very tender. Add more stock if the mixture gets dry during cooking.

Mix the cream with the mustard, add it to the pot and bring almost to a boil.

Watchpoint: boiling spoils the flavor of the mustard.

Discard the bouquet garni, taste the sauce for seasoning and sprinkle with chopped parsley just before serving. Serve the rabbit with mashed potatoes.

Boeuf à la Mode
(Beef Braised in Wine)

3–3½ lb rump or round roast of beef
2 tablespoons oil
1½ cups red wine
1 calf's foot, washed and split
¼ lb piece of bacon, diced
4 medium carrots, quartered
4 medium onions, quartered
bouquet garni
6 peppercorns
clove of garlic, crushed
salt
3–4 cups stock or water
kneaded butter (made with 2 tablespoons butter and 1 tablespoon flour)

For garnish
6–8 carrots, cut in sticks and cooked à la Vichy (see right)
16 baby onions, braised in wine (see Volume 5)

Perhaps the most popular way to braise beef is with wine 'à la mode'. Boeuf à la mode is equally good cold, when the gravy is chilled until jellied (as with boeuf à la mode en gelée, see right). If you like, the wine, vegetables and seasonings can be used to marinate the meat for 1–2 days before cooking. The meat must be cooked very slowly, never using less than a 3 lb piece of meat.

Method
In a deep flameproof casserole heat the oil and brown the beef well on all sides. Discard fat. Pour in the wine and simmer until reduced by half.

Blanch the calf's foot by putting in cold water, bringing to a boil, simmering 5 minutes, then draining and refreshing. Blanch the bacon for 5 minutes, drain and refresh also.

Add the calf's foot, bacon, vegetables, bouquet garni, peppercorns, garlic and a little salt to the pan and pour in enough stock or water to come two-thirds of the way up the beef. Bring to a boil, skim well, cover the pan and braise in a low oven (300°F) for 3–4 hours or until the beef is very tender when pierced with a skewer.

Lift out the beef and keep warm. Discard any fat from the cooking liquid and strain it into a pan, pressing the vegetables to extract the juice. Boil to reduce to about 1½ cups, then add kneaded butter, a little at a time, whisking until the sauce thickens; taste for seasoning.

Carve the beef in three-eighth inch slices and arrange them, overlapping, down a platter. Coat the meat with sauce and spoon the carrot and onion garnish in small piles or 'bouquets' around the edge of the platter. Serve remaining sauce separately.

Boeuf à la Mode en Gelée
(Braised Beef in Gelatin)

3–3½ lb rump or round roast of beef cooked as for boeuf à la mode (see left)
3½ cups liquid from cooking beef (see method)
1 envelope gelatin (optional)
¼ cup sherry

For garnish
carrot and onion garnish as for boeuf à la mode (see left)
box of cherry tomatoes, peeled
bunch of watercress

Method
Braise beef as for boeuf à la mode but do not boil the liquid to reduce. Let the meat cool to tepid in the liquid. Then lift it out, cover and chill.

Strain the cooking liquid and measure 3½ cups; chill it, preferably overnight. The liquid should be firmly set but if not, sprinkle the gelatin over the sherry and let stand 5 minutes until spongy, then dissolve over a pan of hot water.

Skim the solidified fat from measured cooking liquid and heat liquid until melted. Stir in the sherry, with the gelatin, if used, and let cool.

Cool the beef in ¼ inch slices and arrange on a deep chilled platter. Set the cooking liquid over a pan of ice water and stir until on the point of setting. At once spoon a layer over the beef and chill until set. Arrange the vegetable garnish and tomatoes around the edge in small piles or 'bouquets' and chill thoroughly.

Melt the remaining cooking liquid, stir again over ice water until on the point of setting and spoon it over the beef and vegetables. Chill again

and repeat the coating process, if necessary; the beef should be set in a thick layer of gelatin and the vegetables should be lightly glazed. Decorate the platter with a bunch of watercress just before serving.

Vichy (Glazed) Carrots

For 4 people: in a saucepan put 1–1½ lb carrots, trimmed, peeled and left whole if young, or quartered if large. Add ½ teaspoon salt, 1 teaspoon sugar, 2 tablespoons butter and water barely to cover. Cover and cook until the carrots are tender, remove the lid and boil until the water has completely evaporated, leaving a sticky glaze. Sprinkle with 1 tablespoon finely chopped mint or parsley.

Kneaded Butter
(Beurre Manié)

This is a liaison of twice as much butter as flour worked together as a paste on a plate with a fork. It is added in small pieces to thicken a mixture or liquid (usually at the end of cooking).

Boeuf en Daube
(Beef in Casserole)

3½–4 lb rump or round roast of beef.
1 pig's foot, washed
black pepper, freshly ground
1½ cups stock
½ lb lean salt pork
3 tomatoes, peeled, seeded and chopped
½ cup green olives, pitted and quartered
salt

For marinade
2 tablespoons olive oil
2 teaspoons wine vinegar
2 cups red wine
1 onion, sliced
1 carrot, sliced
1 large bouquet garni
strip of orange rind
2 cloves of garlic, sliced
6 peppercorns
1 whole clove
½ teaspoon coriander seeds or ground coriander

Method
Put the marinade ingredients in a pan, bring slowly to a boil, then let cool. Put the beef in a deep bowl (not aluminum) and pour over the cold marinade. Cover and refrigerate for 2–3 days, turning the beef occasionally.

Take out the beef and strain marinade, reserving the vegetables, herbs and spices. Skim the oil from the surface of the marinade and heat the oil in a deep flameproof casserole. Add the beef and pig's foot and brown both thoroughly on all sides, add marinade and reserved vegetables, garlic, herbs and spices, all tied in a piece of cheesecloth. Season with pepper only, add the stock and bring slowly to a boil. Cover and bake in a low oven (300°F) for 7–8 hours or until the beef is very tender.

Simmer the salt pork in

water for 40 minutes, then drain and cut in cubes (lardons). Add them to the pot after 2 hours' cooking. Add the tomatoes to the pot 1 hour before the end of cooking.

To finish, take out the pig's foot and pull the meat in shreds from the bones with a fork. Return the meat to the daube with the sliced olives; discard the cheesecloth bag.

Take out the beef and set on a warm platter, carving some if you like.

Bring the sauce to a boil, skim off any fat, taste for seasoning and spoon a little sauce over the beef, serving the rest separately. Serve with buttered noodles or spaghetti.

En daube means to braise meat slowly for a long time so it is tender enough to cut with a spoon.

A 'daube' is traditionally provençal but there are many versions as it is popular all over France. In some the meat is marinated before cooking, in others cubes of meat are used instead of a whole piece.

Ratatouille

1 medium eggplant, cut in large cubes
2 medium onions, sliced
3 zucchini, sliced
1 red bell pepper, cored, seeded and sliced
1 green bell pepper, cored, seeded and sliced
3 tomatoes, peeled, seeded and sliced
$\frac{1}{4}$ cup olive oil
$\frac{1}{2}$ teaspoon ground coriander
2 teaspoons basil
1–2 cloves of garlic, crushed
bouquet garni
salt
black pepper, freshly ground

This provençal dish uses many of the local vegetables that are sold everywhere in southern France in huge colorful piles during the summer and fall. It is delicious eaten hot as an appetizer or accompaniment for an entrée, or chilled as a salad.

Method
Sprinkle the eggplant with salt, let stand 30 minutes to draw out the juices (dégorger), then rinse with cold water and dry on paper towels.

In a flameproof casserole heat 2 tablespoons oil and fry the onions until soft but not browned. Add the eggplant, zucchini, red and green peppers, coriander, basil, garlic, bouquet garni, seasoning and remaining oil. Cover the pot and cook gently on top of the stove or bake in a moderate oven (350°F) for 30 minutes.

Add the tomato, stir well, cover and cook 20 minutes longer or until all the vegetables are tender but not soft. Discard the bouquet garni, taste for seasoning and serve hot or cold.

Endive Ardennaise

6–8 heads of Belgian endive
2 slices of cooked ham, cut in strips
2–3 tablespoons water
squeeze of lemon juice
mornay sauce, made with 2 tablespoons butter, 2 tablespoons flour, 1$\frac{1}{2}$ cups milk, $\frac{1}{3}$ cup grated cheese (Gruyère and Parmesan mixed or dry Cheddar), $\frac{1}{2}$ teaspoon Dijon-style mustard, salt and pepper
2 tablespoons grated Parmesan or Gruyère cheese
1 tablespoon melted butter

Method
Trim the endives and discard the outside leaves. Put them in a buttered flameproof casserole with the water and lemon juice, cover with buttered foil and the lid and cook over low heat for 5–6 minutes. Bake in a moderate oven (350°F) for 1 hour or until very tender.

Transfer the endives to a heatproof platter, stir the ham into the mornay sauce, taste for seasoning and spoon over the endives. Sprinkle with the endive mixture, grated cheese and melted butter and brown under the broiler before serving.

Navets Braisés (Braised Turnips)

4–6 (1$\frac{1}{2}$ lb) small white turnips, quartered
kneaded butter, made with 2 tablespoons butter and 1 tablespoon flour

For braising
2 tablespoons butter
1 onion, diced
1 carrot, diced
2 stalks of celery, diced
1$\frac{1}{2}$ cups stock
2 teaspoons tomato paste
bouquet garni
salt and pepper

Serve with duck, pork or game.

Method
In a shallow flameproof casserole heat the butter, add the onion, carrot and celery, cover and cook gently for 5–7 minutes until the butter is absorbed. Lay the turnips on top, add the stock, bouquet garni, tomato paste and seasoning. Cover and braise in a moderate oven (350°F) for 30–40 minutes or until the turnips are tender.

Transfer the turnips to a serving dish and keep warm.

Strain the cooking liquid into a saucepan and bring to a boil. Add the kneaded butter, a piece at a time, whisking until the sauce thickens. Taste it for seasoning and spoon over the turnips.

Cabbage Stuffed with Chestnuts

1 firm head of green cabbage
1 lb chestnuts, skinned
1 onion, sliced
2 tablespoons butter
3 cups well-flavored stock
about $\frac{3}{4}$ cup brown sauce or gravy

Serve with game or pork.

Method
Set the oven at moderate (350°F).

Trim the cabbage, removing the outside leaves. Cook it in boiling salted water for 5 minutes, drain and refresh.

Put the chestnuts in a pan with the onion, butter and 2 cups stock. Cover and cook gently for 25–30 minutes or until the chestnuts are almost tender and the liquid has evaporated.

Cut a deep cross in the cabbage, curl back the outer leaves, cut out the center and fill with the chestnuts. Reshape the cabbage and fit it into a buttered casserole. Pour over the remaining stock, cover and bake in heated oven for 45–50 minutes. Spoon over the brown sauce or gravy and return the cabbage to the oven for 5–10 minutes longer.

To Skin Chestnuts

Pierce each nut with a pointed knife.

In a saucepan cover the chestnuts with cold water, bring to a boil and take from the heat.

Lift the nuts from the water with a slotted spoon. Hold them with a cloth and strip away the shell and inner skin with a small sharp knife. If the skin does not peel easily, put back the nuts in the hot water for 1 minute longer.

Ratatouille, eaten hot or cold, is a delicious provençal vegetable dish

Oeufs à la neige (snow eggs) are meringues

The following two desserts are made from similar ingredients but the results are quite different.

Oeufs à la Neige
(Snow Eggs)

3 egg whites
$\frac{3}{4}$ cup sifted confectioners' sugar
$\frac{1}{2}$ teaspoon vanilla extract
2 cups milk
vanilla bean, split
4 egg yolks
$\frac{1}{4}$ cup sugar
1 square (1 oz) semisweet chocolate, grated, or $\frac{1}{2}$ cup sugar and $\frac{1}{3}$ cup water

Makes 20 'eggs'.

Method
Beat the egg whites until they hold a stiff peak; fold in the confectioners' sugar with vanilla extract to make a meringue. Scald the milk with vanilla bean in a shallow pan.

Shape the meringue mixture into ovals with 2 soup spoons and lower 6–8 ovals into the simmering milk. Poach them carefully for 4–6 minutes or until firm to the touch, turning them once. Lift them out on a slotted spoon and drain on paper towels. Cook remaining meringue mixture in same way.

Strain the milk and use to make vanilla custard sauce with the egg yolks and $\frac{1}{4}$ cup sugar (see right). Chill the custard sauce, pour into a glass bowl and pile the meringue 'eggs' on top. Sprinkle with grated chocolate. Alternatively, cook the $\frac{1}{2}$ cup sugar and water to a golden brown caramel as for the 'floating island', dip base of pan in cold water to stop the cooking and dribble threads of caramel over the 'eggs'. Serve chilled.

Ile Flottante
(Floating Island)

4 egg whites
$\frac{1}{2}$ cup sugar
$\frac{1}{2}$ teaspoon vanilla
$\frac{1}{2}$ cup browned, slivered almonds
2 cups crème à la vanille (vanilla custard sauce)
chocolate nonpareils (for sprinkling) – optional

To coat the mold
2 tablespoons butter and 1 tablespoon sugar, or $\frac{1}{2}$ cup sugar and $\frac{1}{3}$ cup water

Charlotte mold, or soufflé dish (1 quart capacity)

Method
To coat the mold or dish: spread it with the butter and sprinkle with sugar, discarding the excess. Alternatively, dissolve the $\frac{1}{2}$ cup sugar in the water, bring to a boil and boil to a golden brown caramel. Pour the caramel into the mold and turn and tilt the mold so the sides and base are lined with caramel. Set oven at moderately low (325°F).

Beat the egg whites until they hold a stiff peak and fold in the sugar with the vanilla and browned almonds until the mixture is glossy. Put the mixture into the prepared mold or dish and poach in a water bath in heated oven for 20–22 minutes or until firm to the touch. Let the mixture cool.

Watchpoint: if the mixture rises above the top of the mold, push in the sides so the mixture can shrink back into the mold as it cools.

Make the custard sauce and chill it. Pour it into a shallow glass bowl. Carefully unmold the 'island' onto a wide metal spatula held just above the bowl and lower the 'island' into the custard; it should float. Sprinkle with chocolate nonpareils, if you like.

Crème à la Vanille
(Vanilla Custard Sauce)

For 2 cups: in a pan put 2 cups milk, add vanilla bean, split, if using, and infuse for 10 minutes; remove. Add $\frac{1}{4}$ cup sugar. Beat 4 egg yolks in a bowl until light in color, scald the milk and gradually stir into yolks with vanilla extract, if using. Return to the pan and stir with a wooden spoon over gentle heat. When the custard coats the back of a spoon and looks creamy, strain back into a bowl. Sprinkle with a little sugar (this helps to prevent a skin from forming); chill.

Charlotte aux Pommes (Apple Charlotte)

8–9 Delicious or other firm
   dessert apples, pared, cored
   and thinly sliced
¾ cup butter
¾ cup sugar
grated rind of 1 lemon
1 lb firm white loaf, crusts
   removed and sliced

*Charlotte mold (1 quart
capacity)*

Method
Set oven at hot (400°F).
   Melt ½ cup butter in a skillet, add the apples, sugar and lemon rind and cook quickly, stirring, until the sugar is melted. Lower the heat and cook about 15 minutes longer or until the sugar and apple juice have formed a light golden caramel.
   Cut 16–18 fingers of bread to line the sides of the mold, and cut triangles of bread for the base. Cream the remaining butter and thickly butter the mold. Press the bread triangles on the bottom to fit perfectly and then line the sides, overlapping the bread fingers slightly; trim the tops, if necessary.
   Put the apple mixture into the prepared mold and smooth the top. Bake in heated oven for about 40 minutes or until the charlotte is firm — for very juicy apples, extra cooking may be needed. Chill the charlotte.
   To serve, unmold the charlotte on a platter and serve with vanilla custard sauce, or cold apricot jam sauce or Melba sauce.
   To make apple charlotte with tart cooking apples: wipe, quarter and core 10–12 tart apples. Put in a thickly buttered pan, add a strip of lemon rind, cover with buttered foil and the lid and cook gently for 15–20 minutes or until soft, stirring occasionally. Work through a sieve or food mill. Measure the purée and return to the pan with 3 tablespoons sugar for each cup of purée. Cook quickly, stirring constantly, until the purée is thick. Line the mold and bake the charlotte as above.

Charlotte refers to the bucket-shaped mold used for all kinds of mixtures varying from cakes to creams like the famous charlotte Russe and to this apple charlotte recipe. The name is said to come from the old English 'charlet' — meaning custard (mentioned in 'The Form of Cury' cook-book of Richard II in 1390).

Apricot Jam Sauce

For 1 cup: heat 6 tablespoons apricot jam with ¾ cup water and grated rind and juice of 1 lemon, stirring until the jam has dissolved. Bring to a boil, take from the heat and stir in 1 teaspoon arrowroot (mixed to a paste with 1 tablespoon cold water). Heat, stirring, until the sauce thicken. Strain the sauce before serving.

Croquettes de Riz (Rice Croquettes)

⅓ cup rice
1½ cups milk
vanilla bean, split
¼ cup sugar
3 egg yolks
¼ cup cornstarch
1 egg, beaten to mix
½ cup dry white breadcrumbs
deep fat (for frying)
hot apricot jam sauce (for
   serving)

Makes 9–10 croquettes.

Method
Put the rice in a pan with plenty of cold water, bring to a boil and simmer 2 minutes. Drain, refresh and drain again. Return to the pan with the milk and vanilla bean and cook gently for 22–25 minutes or until the rice is tender and most of the milk is absorbed so the mixture is creamy. Stir occasionally to prevent the rice from sticking. Remove the vanilla bean, stir in the sugar and egg yolks and cook, stirring, over a low heat, until the mixture draws away from the sides of the pan. Pile the mixture into ice trays and chill until firmly set.
   Divide the rice mixture into pieces the size of small eggs, shape them into corks or cones and roll them in cornstarch. Brush them with beaten egg and coat with breadcrumbs. Heat the fat to 365°F on a fat thermometer and fry the croquettes, a few at a time, until golden brown. Drain them on paper towels and keep hot while frying the remaining croquettes. Serve at once with hot apricot jam sauce.

Gâteau Lyonnaise au Chocolat

1 lb chestnuts, skinned (see
   page 122)
1 cup milk
1½ cups sugar
¾ cup cake flour
pinch of salt
½ cup butter
8 eggs
½ teaspoon vanilla

For filling
1 package (4 oz) sweet
   chocolate
2 cups heavy cream, stiffly
   whipped
1 tablespoon sugar
6 tablespoons orange jelly

For chocolate glacé icing
6 squares (6 oz) semisweet
   chocolate, chopped
6–8 tablespoons sugar syrup
   or water
3½ cups sifted confectioners'
   sugar
1 teaspoon oil
½ teaspoon vanilla

Three 9 inch cake pans

The region around Lyon, France, is famous for chestnuts. Serves 10–12 people.

Method
Put the chestnuts in a pan with the milk, cover and simmer 20–25 minutes or until very soft. Drain well and work through a sieve or food mill to make fine dry crumbs.
   Set the oven at moderately hot (375°F). Grease cake pans, line each with a circle of wax paper, grease them again, sprinkle with sugar, then with flour and discard the excess.
   Sift the flour with the salt. Warm the butter in a bowl over hot water until it is soft enough to pour but is not oily.

Put the eggs in a large bowl, add the vanilla and gradually beat in the sugar. Set the bowl over a pan of hot water and beat until the mixture is light and thick and leaves a ribbon trail. Take from the heat and continue beating until cool. If using an electric beater, no heat is necessary.

With a metal spoon fold in the sieved chestnuts, then the sifted flour in 3 portions, adding the butter just before the last portion of flour. Divide the mixture evenly between the prepared pans and bake in heated oven for 25–30 minutes or until the cakes spring back when lightly pressed with a fingertip. Turn out on a wire rack to cool.

To make the filling: melt the sweet chocolate on a heatproof plate over a pan of hot water; leave until cool but not set. Divide the stiffly whipped cream into 2 portions, one slightly larger than the other, and fold the cooled chocolate into the smaller portion. Fold the 1 tablespoon sugar into the larger portion.

When the 3 cakes are cold, split them, spread each of the 6 layers with a thin layer of orange jelly, then sandwich with the whipped sweetened cream and reshape into 3 cakes again. Then sandwich these reshaped cakes with the chocolate-flavored whipped cream to form 1 large cake.

To make the chocolate glacé icing: gently heat the chocolate with the sugar syrup or water, stirring until smooth and creamy; bring just to a boil. Let cool, then beat in the confectioners' sugar 1 tablespoon at a time. Add the oil and vanilla, and heat the icing to tepid over a bowl of hot water — it should just coat the back of a spoon. If too thick, add a little water or sugar syrup; if too thin, beat in more sugar. Pour glacé icing over cake, spreading it quickly with a metal spatula to coat the cake completely.

Spread six layers with orange jelly, sandwich these with cream and reshape cakes. Then fill three reshaped cakes with the chocolate-flavored cream to form one cake ▶

After forming one cake, pour over chocolate glacé icing to finish the gâteau lyonnais ▶

Gâteau lyonnaise is cut to show the layers of fillings

KINDS OF ONIONS

It is hard to imagine cooking without onions and the members of the onion family such as garlic, scallions, leeks, chives and shallots.

From earliest times the onion has been highly esteemed. In desert regions it was used as a thirst preventative by travelers and soldiers on the march. The Romans used onions to cure the sting of reptiles. Poultices of onions were made for those with watery eyes and onion juice was given to unfortunates who suddenly became speechless.

Onions vary in flavor depending on how they are cooked — blanching lessens their acidity so they are milder and less likely to curdle soups or sauces containing milk. When fried in butter or oil, they should always be cooked slowly so juice is drawn out; when very soft and transparent their flavor is sweet and mild and it becomes richer when frying is continued until they are golden brown. It is important to cook onions to the stage called for in a recipe.

When buying onions, select those that are well shaped with dry skins; avoid any with green sprouts. A good onion should be free from black spots and have a clear color.

Bronze-skinned yellow onion is all-purpose — it has a strong sharp flavor when raw and is essential for dishes like French onion soup where the flavor should be really pronounced.

Large bronze-skinned Bermuda onion is milder, and relished — raw or cooked — with hamburger; it should also be used for recipes like onion pie where the onion flavor should be subtle rather than strong.

Large Spanish red onion is superb for baking and adds color to salads when used raw.

Small white silver-skin onions are used for boiled or creamed onions and as a garnish in stews, fricassées and blanquettes.

Garlic was part of the daily food allowance given by the Egyptian Pharaoh Cheops to the slaves building his pyramids. It was also given to the Roman soldier to make him courageous.

Garlic is used extensively all over the world. Three varieties are grown — the **Creole** or **American garlic**, with a white skin and a powerful flavor; **Italian garlic** which has a pink skin and many attached cloves; and **Tahitian garlic**, which is the largest of them all.

Garlic is available fresh by the 'head', or in the form of garlic powder, garlic salt, garlic chips and garlic flakes. Fresh garlic has the best flavor and very little is needed — one or two cloves from the 'head' are enough for most recipes.

Chives grow in many American gardens and kitchen windows. Their delicate little green spikes, finely chopped, give an agreeable accent to salads, cooked vegetable dishes, rice, potatoes, scrambled eggs, meat sauces and soup garnishes. Freeze-dried chopped chives are generally available when fresh chives are out of season.

Scallions, spring onions or **green onions** are young onions pulled before the bulbs have formed or can be non-bulbing onions that continue dividing and growing at the base of the plant to make new shoots. Scallions are available all year and should be used within a few days. They are excellent in salads, with cottage or cream cheese, or simply eaten with coarse salt.

Leeks, elegant first cousins to the onion, are known in France as 'the asparagus of the poor' and indeed, leeks lend themselves to most asparagus recipes. They must be washed with great care lest the sand that accumulates between the leaves ruins an otherwise perfect dish. The best way to clean leeks is to pull off a few of the outer green leaves, trim off the white root and cut the green part down to 5—6 inches in length. Slit the remaining green leaves lengthwise and wash well. Leeks can be boiled like onions and served with a cream sauce, or they can be cut crosswise and combined with vegetables such as tomatoes, peas, carrots and fresh limas. They

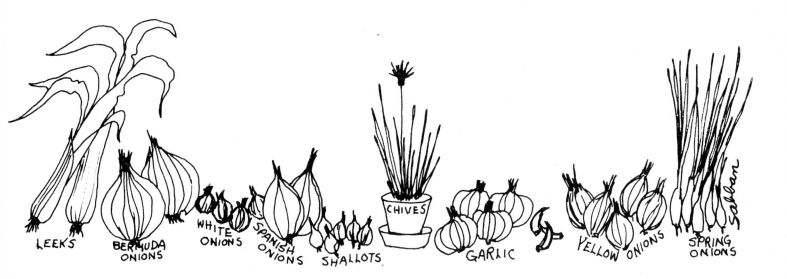

LEEKS BERMUDA ONIONS WHITE ONIONS SPANISH ONIONS SHALLOTS CHIVES GARLIC YELLOW ONIONS SPRING ONIONS

are excellent in soups and stews and as an appetizer or salad, boiled, cooled and then served with vinaigrette dressing.

Shallots, with their gentle flavor and mild aroma, are relatively new in American cooking though they are old favorites in Europe. There is no real substitute for these small, brown-skinned members of the onion family, but the chopped white part of scallions will give a comparably mild onion flavor. In markets where they are available, shallots are sold in small split baskets; they are also sold by mail order, often advertised in home magazines. There is also a freeze-dried shallot powder now on the market. Shallots are a delicious addition to many basic sauces, stuffings, salads, soups and seafood dishes.

Preparation of Onions

To Peel Onion, Garlic or Shallots
If you are peeling more than a few, put them in a bowl of boiling water and let small white onions stand for about 10 seconds or large onions for about 5 minutes; let garlic or shallots stand for about 5 seconds. Drain, refresh and trim both ends. Slip off outer skin and first layer with your fingers. When boiling small white onions, cut a cross in the root end and the onions will keep their shape.

To Slice Onion
Peel onion and cut a thin slice off one side to make a good flat base. Put cut side down on a chopping board, hold onion securely with your left hand with fingers grasping it firmly and slice straight down with a sharp knife, pushing slices away as you cut. To make onion rings: push out the slices into rings.

To Chop and Dice Onion, Garlic and Shallots
Peel onion but leave root end intact and cut in half through the root. Lay cut side down on a board with root end at your left. With sharp chopping knife make a series of cuts down through onion from left to right, cutting just to root but not through it. Then slice horizontally to the chopping board, still leaving slices attached to the root. Finally, cut down crosswise and slices will fall into small pieces. To dice, cut down into large pieces.

To Extract Onion Juice
There are three ways to do this:
1 Cut a slice off the onion and work the onion on a juicer, as you would squeeze a lemon.
2 Cut a slice off the onion. Hold the onion over a piece of wax paper and scrape cut side with a sharp paring knife.
3 Stand a vegetable grater on a piece of wax paper and rub the cut side of an onion on the fine side of the grater.

To Crush Garlic
On a piece of wax paper lay a cut clove of peeled garlic and cover with about $\frac{1}{4}-\frac{1}{2}$ teaspoon salt. With the flat side of a heavy knife, cream or press the garlic until all the fibers are broken down. Or crush it in a garlic press.

To Refrigerate Onions
A good way to save already chopped onions for use later is to put them in a glass jar, screw the top on securely and refrigerate until needed. They will keep up to a week.

To Freeze Onions
Cut raw onions into slices, separate them into rings. Put them on a baking sheet, freeze them and package for the freezer. Small whole onions or chopped onions are best blanched for 2–3 minutes, then drained, before packing for the freezer.

To Remove Onion Odor from Hands
Rub your hands with vinegar, lemon juice or salt. Then wash with soap and water.

Sugar is an important part of our eating pattern. Almost 100% carbohydrate, it is the primary source of energy used by the human body.

As long ago as 1000 B.C., sugar cane was chewed in India because of the sweet taste. Gradually, over a thousand years, sugar moved through the Mediterranean and was brought here by Christopher Columbus. The early colonists had to pay very high prices for their sugar. In fact, it was imported from the West Indies in solid loaves that had to be cut with special sugar shears. Each small piece was worth its weight in gold.

Today the main sources of sugar are the sugar cane and the sugar beet. The completely refined, pure products form the granulated sugar found in all markets.

Brown sugar is made of extremely fine sugar crystals covered with a thin film of molasses. It is this molasses coating that gives the characteristic flavor and color. The most common grades are light brown and dark brown. Another way it is made is by boiling sugar syrup which has not been decolorized. Brown sugar is extremely hygroscopic (it absorbs water readily) and will harden quickly once the package is opened, so store it in an airtight container in the refrigerator.

Cinnamon sugar is a combination of granulated sugar and powdered cinnamon. It is sprinkled over buttered toast, coffeecakes and on cookies.

Confectioners' sugar, frequently called powdered sugar, is granulated sugar that is crushed until very fine and mixed with cornstarch to prevent caking. It is used in frostings, confections, hard sauce, and for sprinkling on baked goods.

SUGARS AND SYRUPS

SABBAN

Corn syrup is a thick, sweet liquid made from a concentrated solution of sugar and the juice of the corn plant. It is available in light and dark varieties and is used over pancakes and waffles.

Golden syrup, a commercial product that comes in a can, is made in England. The process is an industrial secret. The syrup is used in some English desserts and is now available in specialty markets in the U.S.

Granulated sugar is the type most commonly used. It is available as 'Granulated', 'Fine Granulated', and 'Extra Fine Granulated'.

Honey, one of the oldest sweet substances known to mankind, was about the only sweetener until sugar cane was discovered and refined.

Honey is made from the nectar of flowers that honeybees suck and store in their honeysacs. The flowers from which bees gather this nectar determine the color of the honey — usually the lighter the honey, the milder the flavor.

At one time, honey was gathered from wild bees, but since it was the only sweetener, bees were tamed to make their honey readily available. Now bee-keeping has become a hobby, not a necessity, and sweet clover, clover and alfalfa honey make up most of the honey produced.

Maple sugar comes from the sap of the sugar maple trees, concentrated and crystallized into sugar. It is available loose by the lb or in little pressed cakes or molds. Maple syrup is made from the concentrated sap of the same tree.

Molasses is a thick dark syrup obtained in the early stages of sugar refining. It is used in baking and candy-making.

Vanilla sugar can be made in this way: split a 1 inch long piece of vanilla bean; leave it in a jar of granulated sugar with the lid tightly closed. Vanilla sugar is for flavoring fruits, puddings, custards and other desserts, and cakes.

131

MEASURING & MEASUREMENTS

The recipe quantities in the Course are measured in standard level teaspoons, tablespoons and cups and their equivalents are shown below. Any liquid pints and quarts also refer to U.S. standard measures.

When measuring dry ingredients, fill the cup or spoon to overflowing without packing down and level the top with a knife. All the dry ingredients, including flour, should be measured before sifting, although sifting may be called for later in the instructions.

Butter and margarine usually come in measured sticks (1 stick equals $\frac{1}{2}$ cup) and other bulk fats can be measured by displacement. For $\frac{1}{3}$ cup fat, fill the measuring cup $\frac{2}{3}$ full of water. Add fat until the water reaches the 1 cup mark. Drain the cup of water and the fat remaining equals $\frac{1}{3}$ cup.

For liquids, fill the measure to the brim, or to the calibration line.

Often quantities of seasonings cannot be stated exactly, for ingredients vary in the amount they require. The instructions 'add to taste' are literal, for it is impossible to achieve just the right balance of flavors in many dishes without tasting them.

Liquid measure	Volume equivalent
3 teaspoons	1 tablespoon
2 tablespoons	1 fluid oz
4 tablespoons	$\frac{1}{4}$ cup
16 tablespoons	1 cup or 8 fluid oz
2 cups	1 pint
2 pints	1 quart
4 quarts	1 gallon

OVEN TEMPERATURES

Fahrenheit		Level of heat
550°		Broil
450°		Very hot
400°		Hot
375°		Moderately hot
350°		Moderate
325°		Moderately low
300°		Low
200°		Very low

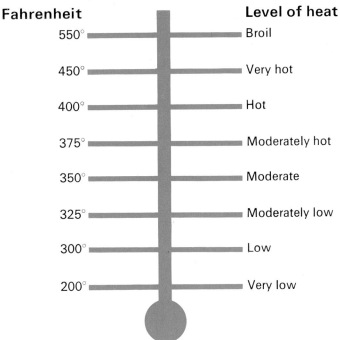

OVEN TEMPERATURES AND SHELF POSITIONS

Throughout the Cooking Course, oven temperatures are stated in degrees Fahrenheit and in generally agreed levels of heat such as 'high' and 'moderate'. The equivalents are shown on the table above.

However, exact temperature varies in different parts of an oven and the thermostat reading refers to the heat in the middle. As the oven temperature at top and bottom can vary as much as 25°F from this setting, the positioning of shelves is very important. In general, heat rises, so the hottest part of the oven is at the top, but consult the manufacturer's handbook about your individual model.

Pans and dishes of food should be placed parallel with burners or elements to avoid scorched edges.

When baking cakes, there must be room for the heat to circulate in the oven around baking sheets and cake pans; otherwise the underside of the cakes will burn. If baking more than one cake in an oven that has back burners or elements, arrange the cakes side by side. If the oven has side burners, arrange cakes back and front.

Oven thermostats are often inaccurate and are unreliable at extremely high or low temperatures. If you do a great deal of baking or question the accuracy of your oven, use a separate oven thermometer as a check on the thermostat.

Cooking Curiosities

In ancient Rome, star dishes at Roman feasts were wild boar, camel and partridge, all cooked on spits over huge open fires. But the delicacies that really tickled a Roman's palate were ostriches whose brains were considered to be the choicest parts.

Medieval times brought about changes. Large spits were turned by professional turnspits or dogs inside a treadmill; and geese were even trained to turn turkeys!

Spits gradually became more sophisticated. In Treviso, an Italian village, the kitchen of Count de Treviso was said to have had a musical spit, that worked like a barrel-organ. It did 130 roasts at a time and played 24 tunes, each one corresponding to different cooking times, so that by the end of the twelfth tune, a fowl was done to a turn.

Today there is the rotisserie with its mechanically-operated revolving spit. The term barbecue grilling is said to have come from Florida, where French settlers spit-roasted goats whole, *de barbe en queue* (from head to tail). Cooking on the spit has turned full circle and even the popular kebab skewer is just another way of roasting.

Michael Holford

Above: spit-roasting as depicted on the Bayeux tapestry
Right: a typical 16th-century Italian kitchen showing two turn-spits (center) and food needed to appease the vast appetites of that time
Below: a dog working a treadmill spit

Radio Times Hulton Picture Library

Radio Times Hulton Picture Library

INDEX

(Volume 6)

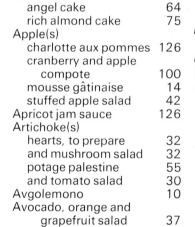

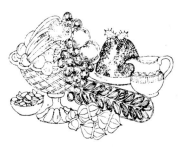
Acknowledgments
Photographs by Fred J. Maroon are on pages 24, 25, 28, 60 and 88. Photograph on page 16 by PAF/C. Délu, on page 39 by Syndication International, on page 46 by Pictor. Other photographs by Michael Leale, John Cowderoy, Roger Phillips and John Ledger. Meat information courtesy of Department of Agriculture, Consumer and Marketing Service, Washington, D.C. and National Live Stock and Meat Board, Chicago, Illinois.

Notes

Notes